Intergovernmental Reforms in the
Russian Federation

Intergovernmental Reforms in the Russian Federation

One Step Forward, Two Steps Back?

Migara O. De Silva,
Galina Kurlyandskaya,
Elena Andreeva, and
Natalia Golovanova

THE WORLD BANK
Washington, D.C.

1818 H Street NW
Washington DC 20433
Telephone: 202-473-1000
Internet: www.worldbank.org
E-mail: feedback@worldbank.org

ISBN-13: 978-0-8213-7967-7
eISBN: 978-0-8213-7968-4
DOI: 10.1596/978-0-8213-7967-7

Library of Congress Cataloging-in-Publication Data

Intergovernmental reforms in the Russian federation : one step forward, two steps back? / Migara O. De Silva ... [et al.].
    p. cm.
  Includes bibliographical references.
  ISBN 978-0-8213-7967-7 — ISBN 978-0-8213-7968-4 (electronic)
  1. Intergovernmental fiscal relations—Russia (Federation) I. De Silva, Migara, 1956-
HJ1211.52.I58 2009
  336.47—dc22

                                                                2009011067

Cover design by Candace Roberts, Quantum Think, Philadelphia, PA, United States
Cover artwork: *En tres tiempos*, Patricia Eyzaguirre. © World Bank Art Program.

Contents

Boxes

Figures

Tables

Foreword

Intergovernmental Reforms in the Russian Federation: One Step Forward, Two Steps Back? is a critical analysis of Russia's intergovernmental reform program which began in the early 1990s. It assesses the effects of a broad range of reforms adopted over two tumultuous decades during which the Russian Federation experienced significant, and at times drastic, political regime changes, coupled with a similarly turbulent economic growth trajectory. This environment reshaped intergovernmental relations, requiring certain fiscal responsibilities to be delegated to the subnational levels. These reforms, however, were not always accompanied by the kinds of administrative and political structures required to support a truly devolved system of intergovernmental fiscal relations. As this study indicates, in recent years there has been a tendency to recentralize some powers that had been granted to subnational governments under earlier reforms—a trend that may call into question the future of fiscal decentralization in the federation. Moreover, the current global economic downturn has had a significant effect on Russia' economic growth, largely because of the country's overdependence on oil, gas, and mineral exports. It is likely that in the present economic climate the political regime will be inclined to further limit subnational autonomy.

As part of the World Bank's Fiscal Federalism and Regional Fiscal Reform Loan and the Regional Fiscal Technical Assistance Project, the World Bank Institute (WBI) designed and implemented a multiyear capacity-building program on intergovernmental fiscal relations which included training and knowledge-sharing workshops in all seven federal administrative districts (*Okrugs*)—from St. Petersburg to Vladivostok. The program yielded several noteworthy publications analyzing the key technical aspects of intergovernmental reforms to date. This book complements the earlier studies and will be of interest to a wider audience including policy makers in developing and transition economies, academics, researchers, and students of Russian affairs.

Sanjay Pradhan
Vice President
World Bank Institute

Acknowledgments

It took almost a year for this study to take its current format, during which we received generous support and encouragement from a large number of people—too many to mention individually. It could very well be that the debt we owe them is as large as the debt of some resource poor–regions scattered across the vast territory of the Russian Federation, the subject matter of this study. The support of several individuals, however, needs to be acknowledged because, as Shakespeare reminds us in King Richard-II, "where words are scarce, they are seldom spent in vain."

First, I would like to convey sincere thanks to my coauthors—Galina, Elena, and Natalia—who patiently endured and responded to my incessant, and always hurried, requests for more information, data, clarifications, and updates. All staff members of Galina's institute (Fiscal Policy Center in Moscow) have, in one way or another, contributed to this study, and we owe them our gratitude. I am also immensely grateful to Barry Weingast (Ward C. Krebs Family Professor of Political Economy at Stanford and Senior Fellow of Hoover Institute) and Ekaterina Zhuravskaya (Hans Rausing Professor of Economics and New Economic School, Moscow, and Academic Director, Center for Economic and Financial Research, Moscow). These two well-known authorities on the subject agreed to review the manuscript amid their extremely busy schedules. We were indeed fortunate to receive their comments and valuable suggestions. I would be remiss if I failed to mention the overall intellectual guidance and support that I received throughout from my colleague and friend, Shahid Yusuf (Economic Advisor), whose detailed comments on an earlier draft of the manuscript greatly enhanced the quality of the final product.

I also would like to thank Sanjay Pradhan, Randi Ryterman, Roumeen Islam, Debbie Wetzel, Robert Ebel, Farrukh Iqbal, Michele de Nevers, Raj Nallari, Anwar Shah, Michelle Morris, Stepan Titov, Valery Ponomarev, Tatyana Leonova, Irina Prusass, Vlada Nemova, Serdar Yilmaz, Igor Zemin, and Indira Iyer for their support at various stages of this project. Stephen McGroarty, Elizabeth Kline, and Nancy Lammers in the Bank's publication unit and Laura Glassman, Barbara Hart, and Linda Stringer of Publications Professionals LLC, made the editing and publication of the manuscript a pleasurable experience. My wife, Chalani, and daughter, Chamari, provided a peaceful environment at home and bore the brunt of my inattention, especially during the last stage of revision and rewriting of the manuscript.

Last but not least, I would like to dedicate this study to my Aunty, Mrs. Chandra Senasinghe ("Sudu Amma"), who is a second mother to all of us—her nephews and nieces.

Migara De Silva
World Bank Institute

About the Authors

Dr. Migara De Silva joined the Bank in 1995 and is currently working as a Senior Economist at the World Bank Institute (WBI). He has designed and managed a number of capacity-building programs in Eastern Europe and Central Asia, East Asia and the Pacific, South Asia, and Latin America regions. He has also managed a multiyear capacity-building program on intergovernmental fiscal relations in Russia, which included all seven administrative regions (*okrugs*) of the Russian Federation from St. Petersburg to Vladivostok. He was the WBI task manager of the joint program with United Nations Development Programme (UNDP) (Bratislava) and the Local Government Initiative of the Open Society Institute in Budapest on Fiscal Decentralization Initiative for Central Asia and the Caucuses. Prior to joining WBI, he worked in the Bank's Development Economics and Evaluation departments and was involved in a wide range of initiatives related to public sector reform. Dr. De Silva has published papers on the impact of resource booms on growth, institutions and economic growth, public sector reforms, and fiscal decentralization in Russia. He co-authored an earlier study with Dr. Galina Kurlandskaya, *Evolving Fiscal Federalism: Russian Practice and International Experience* (Ves Mir Publication, Moscow, 2006), which is widely used by policy makers and researchers in Russia and Central Asia. He holds graduate degrees from the former Soviet Union and United States.

Dr. Galina Kurlyandskaya is one of the most distinguished Russian experts in the field of public finance and intergovernmental relations. She is the Director General of the Center for Fiscal Policy (CFP), a world-known Russian think tank, whose mission is to establish an equitable and efficient system of government finance and intergovernmental relations in transitional economies. She is providing research-based policy advice and technical assistance to central, regional, and local governments in the area of fiscal policy, public finance management, and intergovernmental relations both in Russia and in other developing countries. Dr. Galina Kurlyandskaya received her PhD in Economics from the Institute for World Economy and International Relations, Russian Academy of Sciences.

Elena Andreeva has worked on fiscal decentralization reforms in Russia under many technical assistance projects of the World Bank, U.S. Agency for International Development, U.K. Department for International Development, UNDP and other international donors since mid-1990s. As Research Director of the Center for Fiscal Policy, Moscow, she has worked on many CFP projects aimed at promoting public sector reforms at the federal and subnational levels in Russia and other transitional countries, including the reform of local governance, fiscal equalization reform, and reforms of child welfare. She was one of the authors of the Russian Intergovernmental Reform strategy. She holds a graduate degree from the Economic Department of Moscow State University.

Natalia Golovanova is a lead consultant with the Center for Fiscal Policy (Russia). As a public finance expert, she advises federal, regional, and local governments. She took part in a number of analytical and consulting projects financed by international organizations, including creation of the WBI training program on intergovernmental fiscal relations for regional and local government officials in Russia. She was a member of the analytical team that supported the reform of reassignment of powers across governmental levels in the Russian Federation. She also disseminates the ideas of fiscal federalism through a series of lectures at State University–Higher School of Economics (Moscow), from which she has graduated.

Acronyms

AO	Autonomous Okrug
EBFs	extrabudgetary funds
GDP	gross domestic product
IGFR	intergovernmental fiscal relations
IMF	International Monetary Fund
OECD	Organisation for Economic Co-operation and Development
RF	Russian Federation
VAT	value added tax

CHAPTER 1

Is Fiscal Decentralization Necessary?

A just cause is not ruined by a few mistakes.

—Fyodor Dostoyevsky

Introduction

The Russian Federation is one of the prime candidates for fiscal decentralization. Even following the breakdown of the Soviet Union and the resultant loss of some territories, Russia is still the world's biggest country, stretching across two continents and 10 time zones, from Kaliningrad on the Baltic Sea in the east, to the Bering Strait in the west. Permafrost covers nearly 40 percent of Russia's territory. The remainder includes deserts, tundra, forest, and steppes—with the latter stretching for several thousand miles—as well as high mountains in the south. Russia's immensity and geographic diversity alone are enough to justify the management of the country through some type of a decentralized arrangement. In addition,

The findings, interpretations, and conclusions expressed here are those of the authors and do not necessarily reflect the views of the Board of Executive Directors of the World Bank or the governments they represent. The World Bank cannot guarantee the accuracy of the data included in this work.

the colorful tapestry of multiethnic, multilingual groups constantly attempting to assert their distinct identities adds another layer of complexity. Nowhere else do these challenges combine as acutely as they do in Russia, making the territory largely unmanageable by means of any type of central administrative organ alone.

Beneath Russia's vast territory lie some of the world's most valuable natural resources: about 20 percent of the world's oil, 15 percent of the world's coal, 30 percent of the world's natural gas reserves, 20 percent of the world's nickel, and 25 percent of the world's diamonds come from Russia. Just as the extent of natural resources varies from place to place, the rate of growth of the country's industries varies across regions. Most industries are concentrated in the European part of Russia and in the Urals. This uneven distribution of industrial capacity, which was spawned by historical path-dependencies, adds another layer of complexity to the regional inequality resulting from natural forces. It also poses a major challenge to policy makers who wish to design a viable intergovernmental system without compromising the main objectives of such a system, while simultaneously retaining the country's political and macroeconomic stability. Although an intergovernmental system designed under political expediency is certain to fall short of achieving economic efficiency, a design that ignores political realities is also unlikely to last long. The central difficulty is finding a tacit balance through bargaining and compromise—a task that is much more difficult in Russia than in most other countries, given the complexity of geographic, ethnic, political, and other factors.

Some authors, such as Prud'homme (1995), have specified conditions under which decentralization may do more harm than good. Those conditions include countries where the central government is relatively inefficient, income differentials between households and regions are large, gross domestic product (GDP) per capita is low, where a lack of urbanization implies that raising local taxes in rural areas is likely to be difficult, and local administrations are susceptible to political capture by local elites. A literal interpretation of this list implies that Russia is a poor candidate for decentralization. Fortunately, the interaction of a more complex set of factors than the ones mentioned here determines the relevance and efficacy of decentralization. Given Russia's vast size, diverse geography, and multiethnicity, no central government could effectively govern the country without delegating major responsibilities to subnational governments.[1] One could also argue that some of Prud'homme's

---

1 An eloquent expression of this dilemma is found in an old Chinese saying: "When the Emperor is far away, a General does not obey all his orders".

conditions, such as low GDP per capita, relative lack of urbanization, and large income differentials between households and regions, are symptoms of a nascent decentralized system rather than reasons to stall reforms that would lead to further decentralization.

Is Fiscal Decentralization Necessary?

The two main objectives of fiscal decentralization are to improve allocative efficiency and to enhance productive efficiency (World Bank 2001). Decentralization allows public services to be organized and delivered in a way that will best match local preferences—that is, it can improve allocative efficiency. At the same time, decentralization can improve productive efficiency by making subnational governments more accountable to their constituents, by reducing layers of bureaucracy, and by granting subnational governments more authority to design and implement strategies that are based on their superior knowledge of local conditions, such as local costs, skill availability, and preferences.

Thus decentralization, broadly defined, gives subnational governments more autonomy to make their own revenue, expenditure, and regulatory decisions.[2] Subnational units are better able to make such decisions largely because of their proximity to local populations, better access to information about local preferences, and greater effectiveness at delivering services locally compared with the central government.[3]

---

2 A number of indicators can be used to measure the degree of decentralization. These indicators include aggregate expenditure and revenue measures, such as the subnational government's share of expenditure as a percentage of total expenditure, the subnational expenditure as a percentage of GDP, and the subnational own-source revenue as a percentage of GDP. For example, the International Monetary Fund's *Government Finance Statistics Manual* (IMF 2001) provides 18 country-level indicators of fiscal decentralization. *Deconcentration*, in which units of the central administration are physically located in regions, is not decentralization. To the contrary, the purpose of deconcentration is to strengthen the central government's control over local government provision of public goods and services. Although deconcentration could potentially increase the autonomy of staffs in regional offices, the hierarchical relationship between the central government and the regions remains in place. As Khaleghian (2003), points out deconcentration is "centralization in disguise." The ultimate goal of decentralization is to devolve powers to subnational authorities to carry out their responsibilities without central control. Some authors have gone even further, arguing that decentralization strategy should include privatization, which removes these responsibilities from the public sector altogether (World Bank 2000).

3 Decentralization also has other benefits. The most important one is that autonomous subnational units can keep the central government at bay by limiting its power to usurp local revenues and territories at will. Harber, North, and Weingast (2003) argue that the lack of

Service provision by subnational units also enhances participation, transparency, and accountability (Shah 2004).

Oates (1972), in his classic study *Fiscal Federalism*, presents a major argument in favor of decentralization on the grounds that not all public goods exhibit the same spatial characteristics to be able to account for the diversity of preferences. For instance, whereas national defense benefits all citizens, other public goods and services, such as regional waterways and management of forestry services, will likely benefit only certain regions. Some other public goods and services, such as garbage collection and streetlights, will be important at the municipal level, and the specific needs for those goods and services may vary from one municipality to another. For these reasons, the supply of specific public goods should be entrusted to different levels of government, because the central government does not have access to information on the diversity of preferences in each region or locality. According to the subsidiarity principle, a range of responsibilities, not just service delivery, could be delegated to subnational governments, because taxing (revenue), expenditure, and regulatory responsibilities should be vested in the lowest levels of government except when a convincing case can be made otherwise.[4] In effect, therefore, the provision of public goods solely by the central government will be costly, because its one-size-fits-all approach will often lead to some regions consuming either more or less than they would otherwise have preferred (Tanzi 1995).[5]

Another compelling argument for decentralization is that proximity to local residents and frequent interactions between local government officials and the local population help to forge channels of communication that allow community members to regularly express their opinions. In turn,

---

well-established decentralized political systems in Sub-Saharan Africa has been a major cause of the continent's poor economic performance. Their conclusions are in line with Buchanan's leviathan hypothesis, which argues that fiscal decentralization poses an effective constraint on the behavior of revenue-maximizing governments. The most obvious indicator of this situation is a change in the overall size of the public sector, which, according to Brennan and Buchanan (1980), should decrease with fiscal decentralization, because fiscal decentralization increases competition among local governments.

4 Oates (1972) similarly argues that each public service should be provided by the jurisdiction having control over the minimum geographic area that would internalize the benefits and costs of such provision. For a more comprehensive treatment of this topic, see Shah (2004).

5 Oates (1972) provides four criteria to consider when assigning specific responsibilities to various levels of government: economies of scale, heterogeneity of preferences, externalities (spillover), and competition (emulation), whereby best practices may emerge as a result of several units being involved in the same activity and competing with each other.

such regular interactions and open exchanges make subnational units more accountable to their constituents. At the same time, however, officials in subnational units are susceptible to political capture unless appropriate institutional mechanisms, such as independent audits, public disclosure, and participatory decision-making arrangements (for example, participatory budgeting), are put in place. The main argument for devolving power to lower levels of government is that such administrative autonomy creates an environment where learning, innovation, community participation, and the requisite changes in local administrations can occur so that lower levels of government can respond effectively to local needs (Khaleghian 2003). The anticipated outcome of decentralization would thus be an overall improvement in governance. As some others have argued, decentralization could be a catalyst for democratization because it facilitates and enhances local participation in political decision making (Fiszbein 1997; Rossi 1998).

In developing and transition economies, a rationale for central government to hold power over key fiscal instruments such as taxes, expenditure, and borrowing is to allow the central government a greater degree of flexibility in responding to macroeconomic crises. As some have argued, however, with hard budget constraints and elected local governments, budget deficits may actually become smaller in a decentralized setting (Bahl 1999). Even in settings where interventions by the central government can be justified, allowing subnational governments to play a larger role could minimize transaction costs and greatly improve citizens' access to information (Bardhan 2002). Others have argued that decentralization could both preserve and promote the development of markets (McKinnon 1997; Weingast 1995).

Recent literature has highlighted a number of other virtues of decentralization. For instance, North (1990) points out that an institutional structure such as decentralized decision making is better positioned than a central authority to explore alternatives to solving problems by encouraging trials and eliminating errors. When local authorities provide public goods, some local jurisdictions may discover better ways to provide certain services and others will emulate them. At the same time, transferring responsibilities to those local units that are best positioned to make the desired changes is important. For instance, in some Central American countries, the decentralization of management responsibilities from central to provincial and local governments had little effect on primary education, but when these responsibilities were transferred directly to the schools, education performance improved significantly (World Bank 2000).

Decentralization is an important surrogate for competition, especially in providing public services. The local taxes constituents pay should reflect the quality of local services they receive. In other words, net fiscal benefits, or the difference between taxes paid and the quality of public services received, should be the criterion used to evaluate horizontal equity—and not just the tax rates. Net fiscal benefits account for the difference in tax rates and commensurate benefits in terms of public services across subnational units, where voter preferences for different services also vary.

A disparity between taxes paid and benefits received is a clear indication that the condition of allocative efficiency has not been fully met. Ideally, the outcome of allocative inefficiencies should be that individuals will move to another jurisdiction (they will "vote with their feet") that provides services that better match their preferences (Tanzi 1995; Tiebout 1956). Such movements could, however, have important implications for subnational government revenues. A tax base that is mobile will likely shrink dramatically in response to a tax, and subnational governments will then (in theory) have more difficulty raising revenues than does the central government (Rao and Singh 2005). In reality, movements across jurisdictions are difficult in most developing and transition economies, in large part because of the associated costs involved. In many transition economies such as Russia, the underdeveloped real estate market makes voting with one's feet a virtual impossibility. Some scholars, such as Break (1967) and Strumpf (1999), also point out that inter-regional competition in these economies may lead to the underprovision of some public services and basic infrastructure in some regions and could thereby reduce growth.

Despite these difficulties, the advantages of decentralization are clear, and attempts by central governments to retain their control over subnational governments will have to be reduced over time, especially in countries such as Russia. Many have argued that one way to ensure local autonomy is to allow local governments to elect their own officials, such as mayors and governors, rather than having the central government appoint them (box 1.1). The main rationale for this is that ensuring local autonomy helps promote more widespread democratic institutions, which are then reinforced by decentralization (Tanzi 1995).[6]

---

6 A recent study by Daniel Treisman (2007) critically examines this argument for greater political decentralization as part of decentralization reforms and finds little evidence to support it in the context of recent experiences of developing and transition economies. Although the importance of devolving greater political, administrative, and fiscal powers

Box 1.1

Appointing versus Electing Local Officials

In an influential paper, Blanchard and Shleifer (2000) compare the decentralization outcomes of two countries in transition, China and Russia. They argue that China's high degree of political centralization keeps local governments in line and constitutes an important ingredient that Russia lacks and that has contributed to China's recent development. Blanchard and Shleifer argue that political centralization can take different forms, such as the creation of national parties that can link candidates to a national agenda that all party members subscribe to. They go even further to say that the central government's ability to appoint local officials in China, as opposed to Russia's system of electing them, has given the Chinese government the power to reward or punish local officials who do not subscribe to the central government's pro-growth strategies. In Russia, the relative independence of government officials from such direct control allowed them to pursue goals that increased private benefits at the cost of pro-growth policies.

The Chinese local governments have played an active role in promoting the growth of new firms, which, in turn, have contributed significantly to the country's growth. In contrast, Russian local governments have done precisely the opposite by erecting various obstacles to new firms through taxation, regulation, and corruption, thereby playing the role of "grabbing hands" and restricting growth opportunities for private businesses (Frye and Shleifer 1997). Party-free gubernatorial elections in Russia provide another example of the relative independence of local officials from strictly aligning with a national strategy pursued by the central government.

(continued)

---

to subnational governments remains a sacrosanct goal of decentralization, an interplay of a multitude of other factors—the timing of reforms and implementation strategy in each country; the paths that each process will take once it is set in motion; and the slow emergence of a credible and enhancing institutional setup, political support, and administrative capacity, to name few—makes these reforms far more complex and challenging than is initially assumed. These complexities and challenges could, in some cases, lead to outcomes that are negatively correlated with goals and objectives of reforms. It is, therefore, both far too early and even impossible to downplay the relevance of political decentralization without altering the fundamental assumptions on which the argument for greater devolution of powers across governments rests. Moreover, as Bardhan and Mookherjee (2006: 4) point out, "apart from actual outcomes in terms of policies, their detailed implementation, and their impact on economic well-being, *popular participation is valued for its own sake for variety of reasons.* It can promote a sense of autonomy in citizens, enhance social order by promoting the legitimacy of the state, and limit pressures for separatism by diverse regions and ethnic groups."

Box 1.1 *(Continued)*

Although Prud'homme (1995) does not directly make the same argument, he presents the case of the Republic of Korea as an example, where the first local elections were organized only in 1995. Before that, the central government appointed all mayors, and local autonomy barely existed in Korea, which is regarded as one of East Asia's "miracle" economies.

The situation took a drastic turn when Vladimir Putin came into power. President Putin soon embarked on a plan that will take Russia back to its prereform era. At a special meeting of regional and federal officials held on September 13, 2004, in a swift move to consolidate the central government's power, Putin announced that in place of direct elections, regional parliaments would henceforth ratify Russia's governors on the recommendation of the president of the Russian Federation. This move is widely seen as one that will undermine the multiparty system and earlier intergovernmental reforms that granted greater autonomy to subnational units. Arguably, this change was warranted by more than a desire to address the issue of a weak center. While strengthening the weak center, Russia failed to include "appropriately defined limits on the central government" (De Figueiredo and Weingast 2001), thereby making the central government "too strong" and literally giving the center *carte blanche* to change rules and extracting rents from its regions.[7] Unlike during the "parade of sovereignty" in the early 1990s, when bringing Russia's regions in line to better cooperate with the center required not only a strong center but, ironically, the simultaneous imposition of credible limits on the center to provide incentives for regions to cooperate (Martinez-Vazquez 2002), the recent move toward recentralization was carried out largely without similar safeguards in place.

---

7 Interesting historical parallels can be found in early attempts to limit the powers of a central government (including monarchy). Such efforts were amply rewarded a few decades later in what could be called the critical turning points of the country's destiny. One classic example is the aftermath of the Glorious Revolution of Britain in 1688, which led to the establishment of a representative parliament with a central role assigned to it alongside the Crown and an independent judiciary. Immediately after the revolution, the Treasury Board was established to keep account and control of state revenues and disbursements. A number of sanctions established at the time precluded government departments from making disbursements without prior approval of the Treasury. A practice of farming out certain taxes existed at the time. The total cancellation of such tax farms, including the customs farm, excise farm, and hearth farm, gave the Treasury control not only over expenditure but also over revenue.

In contrast, France still operated under the direct control of the monarchy, which had enormous powers over the country's regions and was thus able to raise taxes and collect a large amount of tax revenues at will. In the long run, having a monarchy with largely unconstrained powers impaired France's ability to maintain its powerful position in

Despite the numerous virtues of fiscal decentralization, its outcomes have not necessarily been unequivocally positive. By itself, fiscal decentralization is neither beneficial nor harmful. When designed and implemented badly, fiscal decentralization will reduce welfare and pose serious challenges to macroeconomic stability, as in the case of the Philippines, where the central government is required to share nearly 50 percent of its tax revenues with subnational governments. This kind of commitment limits the central government's ability to adjust fiscal policy to respond to macroeconomic shocks (World Bank 2000). When done well, fiscal decentralization can improve welfare by increasing citizens' participation in the decisions that affect them and policy makers' real challenge is therefore to figure out how to design and implement fiscal decentralization reforms well (McLure 1995).

Much of the discussion on whether fiscal decentralization is beneficial resembles the debate about whether capitalism is preferable to socialism. As one astute commentator points out, Marxist economists had an easy way out in proving the superiority of socialism: they compared actual capitalism with ideal socialism. Similarly, recent discussions about the efficacy of decentralization compare the outcomes of actual centralization with those of an ideal decentralized system (Prud'homme 1995).

The efficacy of intergovernmental reforms depends in part on the objectives pursued by different levels of government—that is, whether they are social welfare maximizers, leviathan self-seeking bodies, or Niskanen-type bureaucrats. If subnational governments are of the latter two types, decentralization will probably not lead to economic growth (Martinez-Vazquez and McNab 2003). Some have also argued that income redistribution is less easily achieved in highly decentralized states (Ter-Minassian 1997). Although those concerns have some merit, the danger exists that they can be overemphasized as a pretext for withholding fiscal decentralization reforms. As some recent studies have indicated (Shah 1998, 2004; Shah, Thompson, and Zou 2004), contrary to common misconceptions, decentralized fiscal systems offer a greater potential for improved macroeconomic governance than centralized fiscal systems.

Europe. Since French monarchs were much less constrained, the administrative system that they adopted for revenue collection and other purposes lacked the accountability of its British counterpart. The British Treasury was accountable to the parliament and not to the Crown. Furthermore, the British parliament severely limited the Crown's ability to alter rules without parliamentary consent. Such safeguards enhanced the credibility of the government in the eyes of its citizens and particularly its wealth owners. In France, however, such safeguards either were entirely lacking or failed to have a significant influence.

Even in a country such as Russia, where the case for introducing fiscal decentralization is compelling, the underlying principle for introducing intergovernmental reforms should rest on their ability to improve overall fiscal management. This objective can be achieved only when the requisite institutional mechanisms and key political and administrative reforms are introduced as part of the reform package.[8] These institutional mechanisms should promote greater transparency and accountability in relation to fiscal management at all levels of government and should impose hard budget constraints. They should also include clear and distinct rules and procedures to limit moral hazard and free-rider problems.

Although it is easier to provide a list of key institutional measures, establishing a network of workable institutions to reinforce intergovernmental reforms is much harder in practice, largely because some institutions are easier to establish, while others take a long time to ferment and fully embed.[9] The relatively long time horizon it takes for rules, procedures, and other institutional measures to become integral and mutually reinforcing parts of a system of intergovernmental relations could pose a great challenge, including the potential derailment of some of the key reforms

---

Ironically, France's inability to create an effective centralized administrative system was the key to its humiliating defeat in the Seven Years' War with Britain and led to the financial peril it experienced until after the French Revolution (North and Weingast 1989). The British Crown was able to borrow large sums of money from wealth owners because of the credibility it had established through safeguards; however, the French monarchs lacked such easy access to funds. The credible centralized administrative system of Britain allowed the Crown to raise large sums of money for the war through borrowing, which it would not have otherwise been able to do by simply raising taxes. Financing wars through national debt became a new and effective way of raising capital. Since parliament constrained the actions of both the Crown and the chief ministers, debt financing was both easier and quicker. Unfortunately, the French monarchs lacked such abilities to raise large sums of money at short notice and paid the ultimate price of reducing the country to a second-rate military power, albeit temporarily, in the region.

8 The term *institution* is used to describe both formal and informal rules of the game (North 1990) and includes procedures, conventions, edicts, laws, and sets of beliefs. Institutions are distinctly different from *organizations*, even though some authors use the term *institutions* to describe organizations. Organizations ("players") operate within a specific institutional structure or rules of the game.

9 As Yusuf (2009: 60) points out, "except for the simplest ones, institutions are difficult to tailor, to embed, and to develop to a functional level. Carpentering institutions is not simply a matter of following rules because there are no straightforward instructions."

during this gestation period. Therefore, designing and implementing intergovernmental reforms requires the prescience of an inevitability of such outcomes. It also requires relentless political support and administrative capacity throughout the process to allow proper sequencing of reforms and a concomitant alignment of various institutional measures to reinforce these reforms.

Some of these factors are highlighted in Bardhan and Mookherjee (1998), where they identify a set of necessary and sufficient conditions for decentralization that will lead to "superior" (welfare-optimizing) outcomes. These outcomes include a functioning local democracy, adequate fiscal autonomy for local governments, an absence of intercommunity externalities in service provision, and administrative and technical expertise in local and national government officials (in particular in terms of having equal access to and bargaining power over service providers that they have to procure). Thus, the outcome of decentralization reforms depends both on the context where it is implemented and on the way it is designed (Bardhan and Mookherjee 2006).

A poorly designed fiscal decentralization package could be just as bad as the centralized system it aims to replace. A badly designed decentralized system (that is, a set of reforms that squarely focuses only on some form of revenue assignment, such as revenue-sharing arrangements between the center and local governments) gives rise to the possibility of macroeconomic instability and a significant loss of resources, political support, and social stability. The failure caused by the introduction of piecemeal reforms in lieu of a holistic approach to decentralization reforms is clearly evidenced from the recent experiences of some Latin American countries (Burki, Perry, and Dillinger 1999).[10]

Implementing fiscal decentralization is difficult largely because of the inherent contradiction of simultaneously achieving all three key objectives of efficiency, equity, and macroeconomic stability. As one study points out (World Bank 1996), balancing these objectives is difficult because the objectives themselves are partly contradictory, hence leading to a three-way dilemma. Therefore, choosing the degree of fiscal decentralization

---

10 As previously noted, critical political and administrative reforms are necessary ingredients for a successful decentralization, because decentralization involves more than what are traditionally thought of as the pillars of fiscal decentralization (assignment of responsibilities, transfers, borrowing and so forth). On the contrary, decentralization also encompasses the devolution of some political and administrative powers to subnational governments (Martinez-Vazquez 2007).

allowed within a given country is largely a political decision. Take the case of improving equity through equalization grants. These transfers, often referred to as *Robin Hood taxes*, are intended to reduce horizontal imbalances—that is, to give all subnational units a level of fiscal capacity that allows them to deliver a minimum level of services at a certain cost to all their residents. If horizontal imbalance is to be resolved in the same manner that is used to address vertical imbalance (that is, through a gap-filling mechanism), it will require large transfers, which should be adequate to equalize not only the revenues but also the *actual* expenditures of each subnational government. Such "fiscal dentistry" does not make much sense (Rao and Chelliah 1991), because raising the per capita income of all subnational governments to the level of the richest one (that is, trying to achieve interpersonal equity) should not be confused with the objective of reducing interregional inequity, which is one of the main goals of fiscal decentralization reforms (Bird and Tarasov 2002).

The anticipated outcome of equalization grants is to eliminate the possibility that individuals from poor regions will pay a higher percentage of their incomes to receive the same level of services as individuals in rich regions. For example, localities with a higher proportion of children will require proportionately greater expenditure on education (Boadway, Roberts, and Shah 1994). Because subnational governments have different fiscal capacities, they are unable to provide the same levels of public services at the same tax rates: the amount of per capita revenue raised from each region varies because tax bases differ significantly from region to region. Most decentralized fiscal systems incorporate equalization grants from higher levels of government to lower levels to address such imbalances across regions or subnational units. Vietnam provides a classic example. Even though the average per capita income of low-income provinces in Vietnam is only 9 percent of that of richer provinces, expenditures in low-income provinces amount to 59 percent of the expenditures in rich provinces because of transfers from the central government (World Bank 2000).

Central governments will face a serious dilemma when attempting to reconcile the equity objective by reducing horizontal imbalance with the objective of achieving macroeconomic stability through the reduction of vertical imbalance. The only way to achieve both these objectives is by increasing the centralization of the tax base; however, centralization of the tax base will reduce the fiscal autonomy of subnational governments, an outcome that contradicts the objective of achieving greater efficiency through fiscal decentralization. Similarly, simultaneous achievement of local autonomy and macroeconomic stability through reduction of the consolidated fiscal deficit (vertical imbalance or "fiscal gap") could occur only at the expense of promoting greater equity through the reduction of horizontal imbalances.

Because the tax base is unevenly distributed, especially in a country of Russia's size, the decentralization of taxes will give richer regions an advantage over poor regions. One advantage of tax autonomy is that it could "address in a permanent way the difficult problem of vertical imbalance" (Martinez-Vazquez 2007). However, it could lead to larger horizontal fiscal disparities, especially in cases where the geographic distribution of economic activities is unevenly spread across the country. While an uneven distribution of resources provides a strong case for equalization, an attempt to increase equity through decentralization of the tax base would likely cause a "regionalization" of fiscal surpluses and a "federalization" of deficits, thus leading to a large vertical gap and macroeconomic instability (World Bank 1996). The likely outcome under those circumstances is that rich regions would benefit from both lower tax rates and higher revenues because they would be able to finance their expenditure needs more easily than would poor regions. Poor jurisdictions would experience the opposite because it would require more tax effort on their part to provide the same level of services for their residents.[11] The overall impact would be either a continuation or a worsening of existing regional inequities, because the federal transfers will be correspondingly reduced (World Bank 1996). The unilateral adoption of other alternatives, without considering the need for appropriate trade-offs, will lead to similarly unsavory outcomes (table 1.1).

---

11 This dilemma provides a justification for adopting an asymmetric tax assignment in certain cases where larger subnational governments with more revenue capacity are provided a greater degree of tax autonomy than smaller subnational governments whose revenue-raising capacity is significantly weak. These smaller subnational governments would be expected to grow into a greater role over time (Bird and Ebel 2007). However, as Freinkman and Plekhanov (2009) point out, that although asymmetric decentralization may have its benefits, it could suffer from inherent problems associated with the central government's ability to obtain credible information at subnational levels, such as dealing with the demand for regional and municipal projects and the associated costs. Moreover, the lack of widespread support of the local citizens for and the weak accountability of centrally appointed bureaucrats could further compound the problems. A better alternative might be to encourage *intraregional* fiscal decentralization, that is, devolution of funds and responsibilities from governments of rentier regions toward municipalities.

Table 1.1   Fiscal Decentralization: Triangular Dilemma

Objectives	Outcome
• Macrostability (through the reduction of vertical imbalance) • Greater equity (through the reduction of horizontal imbalance) • Greater local fiscal autonomy (leading to higher allocative efficiency) • Macroeconomic stability • Greater local fiscal autonomy • Greater equity across regions (reduction of horizontal imbalance)	• Both objectives could be achieved by recentralizing the tax base. However, recentralization of the tax base will reduce fiscal autonomy of subnational units and will hamper allocative efficiency • Widening horizontal imbalance—that is, increasing inequity across regions • Worsening macroeconomic stability

Source: Authors.

The difficulty of balancing all three objectives makes fiscal decentralization a highly political act; therefore, its success depends as much on political and institutional choices as on technical choices, such as tax rates or formula-based transfers. Indeed, Prud'homme (1995) contends that because decentralization policy has a higher political content than most other policies, the way it is implemented, the different forms it takes, the sequencing of decentralization, and so on determine its success as much as—or even more than—the substance of the policy. Initial conditions matter just as much, especially in many transition economies, including Russia, where some of the essential ingredients for success—institutional and administrative capacity, good governance, accountability, and some of the basic democratic processes such as free and regular elections, to name a few—were initially lacking. In light of all these complexities, the extent of decentralization feasible in a given national context varies. In some cases, political compromises can be made to adopt more comprehensive reforms within a short span of time, whereas in other cases, such compromises may have to be more gradual or may not be feasible at all in the foreseeable future.

A second-best option of determining the extent of decentralization that is feasible within a particular country entails uneven trade-offs in favor of one policy goal over another. These trade-offs depend largely on the initial conditions under which reforms are introduced, and as these conditions change, the pattern of trade-offs will also take new forms. The literature on dynamic changes in initial conditions and the concomitant transformation of the pattern of trade-offs is sparse. Although theorizing about this relationship is difficult, understanding some of the key implementation challenges, such as the sequencing of reforms, the formulation of transfers, the assignment of revenue and expenditure responsibilities to various levels of government, and the introduction of some degree of political and administrative autonomy for subnational governments, is important. A more pragmatic approach to fiscal decentralization reforms is, therefore, to start with realistic goals and strategies and a set of incentives that could align key stakeholders in support of those goals; only then will decentralization reforms gain traction even when the justifications for decentralization are weak.[12]

As mentioned earlier, Russia has diverse climatic, geographic, economic, cultural, and historical conditions. As a result, people in different regions have different preferences for public goods, and the federal government cannot effectively identify priorities for the population of each region. These arguments favor the highly decentralized governance of the country's public sector. At the same time, Russia's regions vary considerably in terms of their tax bases and fiscal capacity, and the large disparity in the regions' economic situations suggests that the federal government should reallocate financial resources. The reallocation function of the federal government's budgetary system becomes even more important because of the uneven economic growth of the regions and the likely changes in their populations in the medium term.[13]

The arguments for and against decentralization require intergovernmental fiscal policy to be flexible enough to provide for a minimum level of public service financing in poorer regions, while simultaneously stimulating economic growth in regions and municipalities with the potential for development. To achieve the optimal balance between these two goals in Russia, the country needs a better assignment of expenditure responsibilities across the federal government, regions, and municipalities and an improved allocation of revenue sources across different tiers of government. At the same time, the structure of the equalization system of intergovernmental fiscal reforms should not create soft budgetary constraints. It should also minimize negative fiscal incentives granted to subnational authorities.

---

12 This recommendation is somewhat opposed to Prud'homme's (1995) argument that if the assumptions on which the justification for decentralization rests are either weakened or destroyed, so too is the case for decentralization.

13 In Russia's case, political considerations—as opposed to efficiency criteria or diverse administrative capabilities across regions—appear to have led to the implementation of asymmetric fiscal arrangements (Martinez—Vazquez 2002).

CHAPTER 2

Administrative and Territorial Divisions

Russia's federal structure is in many ways similar to that of the Russian *matryoshka*, where numerous smaller dolls are completely encased in a larger one (figure 2.1). Although this comparison exaggerates Russia's federal structure, the hierarchical pattern is virtually the same, in that smaller units are "encased" in larger regional and federal structures. As one study correctly points out (World Bank 1996), Russia is a unique blend of a *de jure* federative organization (box 2.1) and *de facto* elements of a unitary state (box 2.2), with an organizational blend that clearly reflects its size, diversity, and communist legacy.

The Russian constitution establishes two levels of government: federal and regional. Local governments form an independent layer of public authority that is not subordinate to the state level of administration.[1] The procedure for establishing government bodies in regions (called *subjects*) of the Russian Federation is determined by a federal law (Federal Law No. 184-FZ on General Principle of the Organization of Government in Subjects of the Federation) that has undergone substantial changes in

---

1 Formally, local governments have separate responsibilities and powers, and they formulate and approve their own budget without the approval of the regional government; however, municipalities find themselves financially dependent on the higher-level government.

Figure 2.1   Russian Federation's Federal Structure

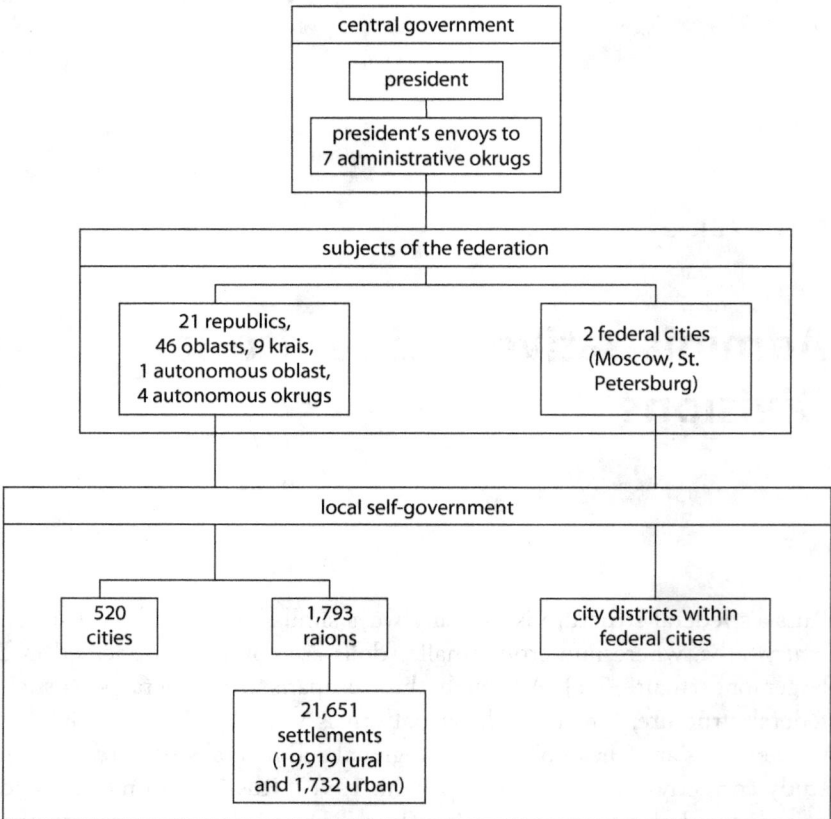

```
                        ┌─────────────────────────────┐
                        │      central government     │
                        │  ┌───────────────────────┐  │
                        │  │       president        │  │
                        │  └───────────────────────┘  │
                        │  ┌───────────────────────┐  │
                        │  │  president's envoys to │  │
                        │  │ 7 administrative okrugs│  │
                        │  └───────────────────────┘  │
                        └─────────────────────────────┘

┌──────────────────────────────────────────────────────────────┐
│                   subjects of the federation                   │
│   ┌─────────────────────┐        ┌─────────────────────┐       │
│   │   21 republics,     │        │   2 federal cities  │       │
│   │ 46 oblasts, 9 krais,│        │    (Moscow, St.     │       │
│   │ 1 autonomous oblast,│        │     Petersburg)     │       │
│   │ 4 autonomous okrugs │        │                     │       │
│   └─────────────────────┘        └─────────────────────┘       │
└──────────────────────────────────────────────────────────────┘

┌──────────────────────────────────────────────────────────────┐
│                     local self-government                      │
│  ┌──────────┐   ┌──────────┐         ┌─────────────────────┐   │
│  │   520    │   │  1,793   │         │ city districts within│  │
│  │  cities  │   │  raions  │         │    federal cities   │   │
│  └──────────┘   └──────────┘         └─────────────────────┘   │
│                 ┌──────────────┐                               │
│                 │    21,651    │                               │
│                 │  settlements │                               │
│                 │ (19,919 rural│                               │
│                 │ and 1,732 urban)│                            │
│                 └──────────────┘                               │
└──────────────────────────────────────────────────────────────┘
```

Source: Authors.

recent years. Among other things, the law establishes a list of responsibilities for bodies of state power of Russian regions and a procedure for conferring power on the chief executive of a subject of the Russian Federation, who is nominated by the president with no alternative candidates involved.

The federal Law on Local Self-Government (Federal Law No. 131-FZ on General Principles of the Organization of Local Self-Government), a new version of which became effective in 2006, establishes principles for the organization of local self-government. Before the new legislation, despite constitutional guarantees for local self-government, localities in many regions were acting as local branches of regional administrations and had minimum decision-making autonomy and no budgets of their own.

Box 2.1

Structure of the Russian Federation

Russia is a federative state with a republican form of governance. The chief executive is the president, who is elected through universal, equal, direct, and secret suffrage for a term of four years. According to the constitution, the same person cannot hold the office of president for more than two successive terms. The parliament is the representative and legislative branch of the government and consists of two chambers or houses: the State Duma and the Federation Council. The State Duma, the lower house, has 450 deputies, who are members of those political parties that successfully passed the 7 percent barrier (7 percent of total votes) at elections. Elections to the duma are held on the basis of universal, equal, direct, and secret suffrage for a term of four years. The Federation Council, the upper house, a standing body, consists of two representatives from each region: one from the representative branch of regional government and one from the executive branch of regional government.

Box 2.2

The Federation Council: A Rubber Stamp of the President?

The influence that the levels of government exert on each other is in practice a one-way street: the federation government largely determines regional policies and not the other way round. The Federation Council, which is supposed to protect regional interests, is in effect defending federal interests. For instance, the Federation Council approved the president's initiative to change the procedure for establishing the Federation Council: governors and speakers of regional parliaments were excluded from membership, thereby substantially weakening the council's political clout. The Federation Council also approved the president's initiatives to change tax and budget legislation, which abolished a number of regional and local taxes and lowered the share of federal taxes going to regional budgets. The members of the Federation Council were almost unanimous in their support of the president's initiative to change the procedure for election of governors, who will be elected not by the citizens, but by each regional parliament, which will vote for a single candidate nominated by the president.

Russia's subnational structure consists of four layers.[2] As of March 1, 2008, the first layer includes 83 regions, which are referred to as *subjects of the federation*. These subjects consist of 21 republics (native territories), 46 oblasts, 9 krais, 4 autonomous okrugs, 1 autonomous oblast, and the 2 federal cities of Moscow and St. Petersburg. According to the constitution, all subjects of the federation have equal rights, but the powers of autonomous okrugs are limited by federal laws. Specifically, the powers of subjects of the federation with respect to the organization of local self-government are limited to procedural matters, such as establishing the boundaries and status of municipalities and fixing a date for the first municipal elections.

Recently, seven federal *okrugs* (federal administrative districts) have been established, which are superimposed on regions to divide the country into seven administrative districts. These federal okrugs are best described as deconcentrated federal government units that are, at least in theory, able to provide some oversight and control over subjects of the federation, although the actual legal status of these units remains largely elusive. As of January 2007, the regions were subdivided into 520 larger cities (known as *gorodskoi okrugs*) and 1,793 rural areas (municipal *raions*). The raions are subdivided into smaller settlements (called *poselenie*), which include towns and smaller rural areas that combine two or three villages. Russia currently has 21,651 such smaller settlements (Federal State Statistics Service 2007). All local government units are theoretically independent of regional governments in terms of their budgetary and administrative status. In practice, however, they depend heavily on regional transfers and regional public investment policies.

The combination of a complicated subnational structure and the great diversity across the subnational units in terms of their ethnic composition, resource endowment, industries, weather, geographic location and conditions, socioeconomic development, and so on poses major challenges in designing an intergovernmental system that can achieve both objectives of equity and efficiency. For instance, in six

---

2 The fiscal system is supposed to consist of three or four tiers, depending on the type of jurisdiction: federal, state (regional), city (or raion level—that is, county level—in lieu of the city level), and settlements within a raion level. Because of the difficulty in implementing a new system of local self-government countrywide, a transition period is in effect until 2009. Currently, local self-government is virtually nonexistent within the federal cities of Moscow and St. Petersburg and consists of only two tiers: federal and regional.

subjects of the Russian Federation, the population does not exceed 75,000, but the geographic size of each is comparable to that of Germany. Similarly, the population of the most densely populated region, even excluding Moscow and St. Petersburg, is 6,000 times that of the least populated region.

Most industries are located in the European part of Russia, such as in Moscow and St. Petersburg and around these cities, along the Volga River, and in the Urals, whereas a large portion of the country's natural and most oil resources are located in Siberia. Khanty-Mansi Autonomous Okrug in Tyumen Oblast in Siberia for instance, accounts for about 1 percent of the country's total population but produces nearly two-thirds of Russia's oil. As McLure (1994a) points out, the ratio of the oil production share to the population share exceeds 70; hence, allowing the region to keep a large share of the revenues from taxes on oil would lead to large fiscal disparities across subnational governments.[3] Few other regions have the advantage of a local revenue base that could cover their expenditures many times over.

The concentration of ethnic minorities is similarly unbalanced. Minorities such as Bashkirs and Yakuts are concentrated in certain geographic areas, and the ethnic-based administrative units, such as the republics and autonomous okrugs, constitute roughly half the country's territory (Wallich 1994). In addition, Russia has a wide diversity of borders, ranging from historical borders that coincide with the boundaries of former Soviet republics; to ethnic borders that coincide with the boundaries of territories populated by particular ethnic groups; to natural boundaries, such as rivers, mountains, and undeveloped territories; to the socioeconomic boundaries of an economic activity zone. This variety adds to the complexity of administration in the world's largest federation.

The complicated administrative division is rooted in the history of Russian territories and the transformations of the political system. Given the upheavals whereby one political division principle gave way to another, the rationale behind existing boundaries is not always clear. Historical boundaries have survived only in the European part of Russia. Beyond the Urals, where many territories remain undeveloped, boundaries tend to be based on geographic features. The borders of the republics are in some cases only theoretically based on ethnic concentrations because the ethnic

---

3 For example, in 1998, the difference between the highest (Tyumen Oblast) and the lowest (Ingushetia Republic) GDP per capita was 18-fold (Martinez-Vazquez 2002).

population often does not constitute the majority of the total population,[4] although in many republics, the size of the ethnic minority is growing. The vagueness of ethnic borders is the source of the Kalmyks' territorial claims against Astrakhan Oblast and the Buryats' claims against the autonomous okrugs of Aginsky and Ust-Ordinsky. The border between the Chechen Republic and Ingush Republic is not clearly delineated even on maps. Regions based on other than ethnic principles also have a list of claims against other regions, such as Krasnodar Krai's reported intention to seize back Adygeya Republic, which had separated from Krasnodar some time ago.

The "parade for sovereignty" during the early 1990s in the wake of the breakup of the Soviet Union induced the ethnic minorities' quest for political and economic independence and resulted in the split of territorial units as formulated at that time and the creation of new subjects of the federation. The economic autonomy of some areas within regions or the close geographic locations of those areas to their neighbors also made the boundaries between them largely arbitrary. For instance, Norilsk, which is not a subject of the federation but an economic area around the city of Norilsk, was the economic center of Taimyr Autonomous Okrug, within which Norilsk existed as an enclave. Formally, Norilsk fell under the jurisdiction of Krasnoyarsk Krai, with which it had no common border but to which Norilsk paid most of its taxes.[5] Other examples are Komi-Permyatsky Autonomous Okrug, which gravitated toward economically and geographically larger Perm Oblast (the two formed Perm Krai in 2005), and Kamchatka Oblast, which formed a similar alliance with Koryak Autonomous Okrug.

The diversity between various areas within Russia clearly hinders the development of symmetric relations between them and the federal government, thus making a case for consolidation through mergers.[6] The first practical steps toward consolidation were taken in 2004, following an

---

4 According to the 2002 *All-Russia Population Census* (Federal State Statistics Service 2004), the title nation accounted for more than 50 percent of the population in only 8 of 21 republics and in only 2 of 10 autonomous okrugs. Even in political heavyweights such as Bashkortostan, Bashkirs account for only 30 percent of the population.

5 Krasnoyarsk Krai, Taimyr Autonomous Okrug, and Evenk Autonomous Okrug formed a new Krasnoyarsk Krai in 2007.

6 Although asymmetric decentralization has some advantages in multiethnic and geographically diverse settings, it could lead to a different set of challenges, as is clear in Russia's case where, asymmetric decentralization led to huge costs. For instance, some of the political trials and tribulations that Russia went through and the resulting outcomes, such as fiscal

Table 2.1   Mergers of Subjects of the Russian Federation

Merging Russian Federation subjects	Name of the new Russian Federation subject	Date of consolidation	Transitional period
Perm Oblast Komi-Permyatsky AO (Autonomous Okrug)	Perm Krai	December 1, 2005	Before January 31, 2007
Krasnoyarsk Krai Taimyr AO Evenk AO	Krasnoyarsk Krai	January 1, 2007	Before December 31, 2007
Kamchatka Oblast Koryak AO	Kamchatka Krai	July 1, 2007	Before December 31, 2008
Irkutsk Oblast Ust-Orda Buriat AO	Irkutsk Oblast	January 1, 2008	Before January 1, 2009
Chita Oblast Aginsk-Buryat AO	Zabajkalsk Krai	March 1, 2008	Before January 1, 2009

Source: Federal constitutional laws.

official decision to merge Perm Oblast and Komi-Permyatsky Autonomous Okrug as of December 1, 2005. The list of areas which have recently merged are given in table 2.1.

Although the governors of relevant subjects of the federation formally proposed these mergers, which had to be approved by referenda, these regional initiatives were an outcome of the federal government's political and financial influence, which it used to push for mergers. One case in point is the federal government's commitment to expand its investment program in Krasnoyarsk Krai and Taimyr and Evenk Autonomous Okrugs for the entire transition period and concurrently to continue providing federal equalization transfers to the okrugs. Similarly, a crude oil exploration program will be undertaken in the newly established Perm Krai that will, for the most part, be financed from the federal budget.

Also on the agenda are possible mergers between Archangelsk Oblast and Nenets Autonomous Okrug and between Stavropol Krai and Karachaevo-Circassian Republic. Other potential candidates for mergers are the richest subjects of the federation, including Yamalo-Nenets Autonomous Okrug, Khanty-Mansi Autonomous Okrug, and Tyumen Oblast. However, in 2004

irresponsibility, economic stagnation, and the absence of a unified legal system throughout Russia—not to mention the country's uneven geographic distribution of resources—could largely be attributed to its asymmetric federalism (Martinez-Vazquez 2002; Polishchuk 2000).

the three subjects signed a treaty that delineated their responsibilities for a term of five years, which means that Yamalo-Nenets and Khanty-Mansi Autonomous Okrugs will remain independent of Tyumen Oblast at least until 2010.

If all those mergers, along with those considered highly unlikely (between Moscow and Moscow Oblast and between St. Petersburg and Leningrad Oblast) take place, the number of subjects of the federation will fall from the current 83 to 74 (89 existed before the first merger),[7] which would still be a record number of territorial divisions for a federative state. Such mergers thus are unlikely to significantly improve the country's manageability. Mergers between regions invariably run into the problem of intergovernmental fiscal relations and distribution of taxes, especially in the case of the mineral extraction tax, on which some regions rely heavily. Thus, regions with scarce mineral resources and insufficient industrial capacity are much more readily talked into mergers than stronger and wealthier regions.

By law, a merger must be preceded by a referendum, which should explain the personal benefits to be derived from a merger in a straightforward manner to every resident. When the residents of a richer region understand that the inevitable consequence will be a drop in per capita budget revenues if they merge with a poorer region, they are unlikely to approve any such merger. Therefore, even though further mergers are possible, they are unlikely to occur on a mass scale.

---

7 The Ministry of Regional Development is discussing the idea of dividing Russia into 23 regions, but any such change is unlikely to take place in the near future.

CHAPTER 3

History of Intergovernmental Relations

The history of intergovernmental relations in Russia helps explain the emergence of its complicated intergovernmental design. The intergovernmental system has been undergoing a series of changes since the early 1990s, and during this period, fiscal decentralization has significantly transformed the country. These reforms were expected to improve the intergovernmental system and macroeconomic stability but have faced significant implementation challenges. Some of the challenges resulted from the inherent nature of such reforms, which required compromises among the many stakeholders. Subnational units whose responsibilities had hitherto been marginalized suddenly found themselves having to undertake more mandates with fewer resources. Regions that were endowed with the bulk of the country's natural resources criticized reforms that would significantly reduce their share of local tax revenues. Some republics, such as Bashkortostan and Tatarstan, unilaterally instituted a "single-channel" tax regime in early 1992, which remitted only a portion of taxes to the federal government, and by 1993, the number of oblasts that had implemented this same measure had increased from 20 to 30 (Litvack 1994). In an effort to acquire more autonomy than they had enjoyed during the Soviet era, a number of regions that lacked any special bargaining powers started to demand more autonomy by seeking the status of republics.

The conditions under which Russia had to reform its intergovernmental system were so unique that traditional approaches recommended in the literature (Musgrave 1959, 1983; Oates 1972; Tiebout 1956) were of limited use.[1] Regional differences may not disappear with economic development,[2] but this possibility should not be taken as a justification for forgoing or postponing intergovernmental reforms. As de Tocqueville (1904) concluded after visiting the United States some two centuries ago, the more decentralized the country, the less authoritarian it is. De Tocqueville's observation resonates well with Russia's recent history of regime change and its current reforms in relation to intergovernmental fiscal relations. As Prud'homme (1995) points out, the worst dictatorships of the past two centuries came out of totalitarian—hence, centralized—regimes; therefore, in Russia, even if decentralization were not that desirable from an economic point of view, it might still be worth decentralizing to ward off the risk of the emergence of a totalitarian regime again.

From the beginning (1992–93), reforms in fiscal federalism were largely driven by macroeconomic concerns. However, equity concerns also provided some impetus to introducing these changes (World Bank 1996). Although a balancing act to find the right trade-off between growth and equity characterized the relationship between the federal government and the regions, intergovernmental relations were influenced more by the need to achieve political unity as opposed to equity. The possibility that rich regions would withdraw resources from the equalization pool was a danger that could only be tempered by adopting a derivation-based arrangement for revenue sharing (Wallich 1994).

Some regions were demanding greater autonomy and even secession from Russia. Two main factors encouraged such behavior. First was the environment that prevailed in the immediate aftermath of the disintegration of the Soviet Union, which provided an opportunity to seek greater independence. Second was the fiscal burden thrust upon the regions with the transfer of little or no matching resources from the federal government. The tax-sharing arrangement that was later introduced came almost as an afterthought and was intended mainly to placate the regions

---

1 Bird, Ebel, and Wallich (1995) make the same observation and argue that the standard approach neglects the role of subnational governments in some critical areas, such as stabilization, safety nets, and privatization, and does not fully address how transition economies should implement intergovernmental reforms in an environment where the legacies of a command economy still lurk beneath the surface.

2 Prud'homme (1995) makes this argument convincingly.

rather than as a genuine attempt to increase efficiency through decentralization.[3] Conversely, the tax-sharing arrangements granted to regions without a proper assignment of expenditure responsibilities could have led to serious macroeconomic instability, as happened in some of the Latin American countries.[4] The greater discretionary spending opportunities granted to subnational governments through extrabudgetary funds have been another key factor influencing their push for greater autonomy (Bahl and Wallich 1995).

In the 1990s, the excessive expenditure obligations of regional governments, including the unfunded federal mandates on the one hand and soft budget constraints on the other, led to an accumulation of overdue liabilities by regional governments. To pay off these liabilities, many regional governments took to accepting in-kind payments of taxes, a move that put the entire budgetary system at risk. To bring the situation under control, the federal government established budget deficit ceilings for subnational governments and took a number of special measures, including debt swaps and mutual settlements of overdue obligations between subnational governments and the private sector. The measures were moderately successful, but they resulted in the growth of unacknowledged government obligations. Those that were mandated by law but were not budgeted for did not contribute to budget deficits. The 1998 financial crisis had a healing effect on the budgetary system, because accelerated inflation reduced the amount of accumulated overdue liabilities of subnational governments in real terms, and the economic growth that followed the crisis permitted them to pay off their obligations. However, the problem of unfunded mandates was not fully resolved until 2005, the year of expenditure assignment reform.

Table 3.1 presents the main stages of development in intergovernmental fiscal relations in Russia.

---

3 Shared taxes could take many forms. They could be a share of central taxes flowing to the subnational government, or they could represent a portion of subnational government taxes whose rate is determined by the subnational government but whose collection is a central government responsibility. In the former case, the sharing of taxes by the central government actually amounts to nothing but an intergovernmental transfer; in the latter case, it is truly subnational because the rate is determined by the subnational government (Bird and Tarasov 2002).

4 For instance, Brazil's 1988 constitution mandated a huge increase in federal tax sharing without any provisions to allow the devolution of spending responsibilities. This situation led to recurrent deficits at the federal level (Burki, Perry, and Dillinger 1999).

Table 3.1   Main Stages in the Development of Intergovernmental Relations

Years	Milestones
1991–93	**Spontaneous decentralization**
	1991: Multilevel budgetary system set up
	1991: Federal Law No. 1550-1 Law *On local self-government*
	1991: Federal Law No. 2118-1 *On the foundation of the tax system adopted*
	1992: Federative Agreement signed by most subjects of the federation
	1993: Federal Law No. 4807-1 *On the foundation of the budgetary rights and the rights to form and use extra-budgetary funds by the bodies of state and executive power of the republics constituting the Russian Federation, autonomous oblasts, autonomous okrugs, krais, oblasts, the cities of Moscow and St Petersburg, and local self-governments* adopted
	1993: Russian Federation constitution adopted
1994–98	**Formalization of the rules**
	1994: Uniform sharing rates for federal shared taxes introduced for most Russian Federation subjects and the Federal Fund for Financial Support of Regions established
	1995: Federal Law No. 154-FZ *On general principles of the organization of local self-government* adopted
	1997: Federal Law No. 126-FZ *On financial foundations of local self-government* adopted
	1998: Budget Code adopted
	1998: Tax Code: Part I adopted
	1998: *Strategy of the IGFR Reform of 1999–2001* adopted
1999–2001	**Further steps in fiscal decentralization and political recentralization**
	1999–2001: Implementation of the first strategy for the Intergovernmental Fiscal Relations (IGFR) Reforms
	1999: Federal Law No. 84-FZ *General principles of the organization of government in subjects of the federation* adopted
	2000: Equalization transfers formula developed; compensation fund for federal mandates established
	2000: System of federal okrugs created
	2000: Provisional methodological recommendations on regulation of intergovernmental fiscal relations for subjects of the federation adopted

2000: Tax Code: Part II adopted

2000: Budget Code came into force

2001: *Fiscal federalism strategy up to 2005 adopted*

2002–04 **Assignment of power and local government reform**

2002: Fiscal federalism strategy up to 2005 implemented

2003: Federal Law No. 131-FZ *On General Principles of the Organization of Local Self-Government* adopted

2004: By Federal Law No. 122-FZ, Federal Law No. 184-FZ (assignments relating to joint jurisdiction of the federal and regional governments), the Budget Code (assignment of revenue sources, transfer allocation system) amended, 150 federal laws amended, 40 federal laws abolished, federal mandates canceled

2004: Governors no longer elected by direct vote; instead they are to be appointed by regional legislatures following a nomination of the candidate by the president of Russia

2005–08 **Fiscal recentralization**

2005: Federal Law No. 122-FZ came into force: responsibilities and powers assigned, federal mandates canceled, benefits monetized

2006: Federal Law No. 131-FZ came into force: new system of local self-governance, transition period for local self-government reform extended until 2009

2006: *The concept for increasing the efficiency of intergovernmental relations and improving subnational finance management in 2006–08 adopted*

Regions merged

Federal government strengthening undertaken

2008: Transition to medium-term planning, changes in the equalization transfer allocation methodology were undertaken

Source: Authors.

Spontaneous Decentralization, 1991–93

With the dissolution of the Soviet Union in December 1991 and the formation of the Commonwealth of Independent States, the political regime was more concerned about achieving macroeconomic and political stability than establishing an effective government structure. Even some of the fiscal reforms undertaken early on, such as transferring expenditure responsibilities to the regions, were carried out primarily for macroeconomic reasons; more specifically, to reduce the central government's fiscal burden. About 17 percent of consolidated government expenditures were transferred from the federal government to subnational governments as indicated by the sharp increase from 1992 to 1993 in figure 3.1. Although this change eased the fiscal burden on the federal government, the transfer of some expenditure responsibilities—such as those for social welfare, for local transportation price subsidies, and for public utilities—created political tension between the federal government and the regions.

Concurrently with the transfer of federal powers to the subnational level, the economy underwent some major transformations: the public sector's share of GDP declined from 52 percent in 1992 to 42 percent in 1994; the campaign to privatize various entities was ongoing; and enterprises were transferring social facilities they had previously owned, such as housing, health care institutions, and educational establishments, to local governments' balance sheets.

Figure 3.1   Share of Subnational Expenditures in Total Outlays of National and Subnational Government without Extrabudgetary Funds, 1992–2006

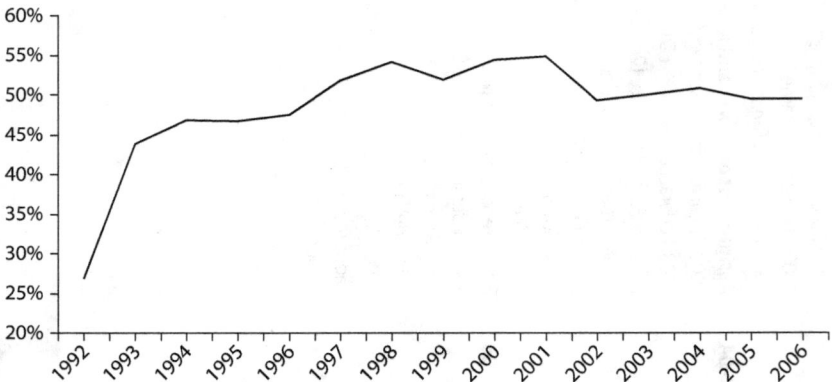

Source: Authors' calculations based on Ministry of Finance data (excluding extrabudgetary funds).

The first elections of governors took place in June 1991 in Moscow, St. Petersburg, and Tatarstan. Elected heads of regions were able to take a stronger position in negotiations with the federal government. Some academics have argued that popularly elected heads of regions significantly weakened the chain of command between the federal government and the regions, thereby preventing the federal government in Russia from pursuing a coherent growth strategy, unlike the government in China (Blanchard and Shleifer 2000). Indeed, federal authorities were forced to negotiate with each of the regions following the elections—in stark contrast with the earlier state of affairs, whereby the federal government dictated terms to subnational authorities (Martinez-Vazquez and Boex 2001).

As a counterbalance to strong regions, the federal government introduced election of heads of local self-governments. The first Law on Local Self-Government (Federal Law No. 1550-1), adopted in 1991, guaranteed elections for the heads of administrations (elections for bodies of the representative branch of government had been granted in 1990 by Soviet law). The new law also dissolved local executive committees, which had been the lowest level of the hierarchy of the state administration. To regulate budgetary issues, the Law on the Basic Principles of the Budgetary System and Budgetary Process was adopted in 1991, and with the 1991 Law on the Foundation of the Tax System, a list of taxes accruing to regional and local budgets was established. However, the federal government regulated the bases and the rates of these taxes and retained the power to collect local taxes.

The 1993 Law on the Foundation of Budgetary Rights and the Rights to Form and Use Extrabudgetary Funds by Bodies of State and Executive Powers of the Republics Constituting the Russian Federation, Autonomous Oblasts, Autonomous Okrugs, Krais, Oblasts, the Cities of Moscow and St. Petersburg, and Local Self-Governments gave subjects of the federation the right to use extrabudgetary funds, which reduced the transparency of the budgetary system. Regional authorities, however, failed to observe many of the provisions of federal laws and regulations (Lavrov 1998).

In 1993, when these laws were enacted, intergovernmental transfers were negotiated between the federal government and individual regions rather than determined according to a uniform formula. Shares of relevant taxes were set separately for each region, and federal subventions covered the budget deficit. In accordance with the annual laws on the federal budget, the regions received subsidies (nonearmarked transfers) to cover the estimated gap between their current expenditures and current revenues, as well as earmarked transfers for capital expenditures. To estimate the gap, the federal Ministry of Finance came up with a regional revenue forecast and estimated regional spending needs. The latter estimate was based primarily on actual collected revenues and reported expenditures and then adjusted during negotiations between the federal Ministry of Finance and each region. The allocations of earmarked capital transfers reflected the political weight of specific regions.

This kind of fiscal regulation provided negative incentives to the regions: the more revenues a region generated, the less federal financial support it received or the lower the proportion of shared taxes (subject to annual revision) it was allowed to retain. In 1994, unified shares of the three major state taxes (excluding the value added tax, or VAT)— enterprise profits tax, personal income tax, and excise taxes—were assigned to consolidated regional budgets for a period of five years.[5]

From the formal point of view, the Federative Agreement—a treaty that most regions signed in March 1992—marked a significant step in the development of fiscal federalism. One of the main objectives of the agreement was to regulate the power struggle between the federal government and the regions; however, strong regions, including national republics such as Bashkortostan, Tatarstan, and Sakha (Yakutia), signed bilateral agreements with the federal government. Some of the republics that refused to sign the treaty received favorable treatment because they were endowed with oil and mineral deposits. In later years, the federal government concluded similar agreements formalizing the asymmetrical devolution of federal powers with other regions.

For instance, by mid 1996, 24 of such treaties were signed, and regions such as Yakutia, which was among the first two regions to enter into a bilateral agreement (Bashkortostan was the other one), sent no tax revenue to the federal government as a result of the agreement of 1992–93. In the case of some other regions, tax remittances to the center reduced over time. In Karelia, the share of federal taxes decreased from 95 percent in 1994 to 67 percent in 1995, and in Tatarstan, it decreased from 84 percent to 77 percent during the same period (Gaidar 1996). The

---

5 As Le Houerou (1994) notes, successive attempts to come up with arrangements for sharing the VAT revenues have not been straightforward. For example, during the first part of 1992, the regions' share of the newly introduced VAT was negotiated on a case-by-case basis, and in 1993, the government settled on a negotiated formula that could vary from 20 to 50 percent, depending on the region. The formula for sharing taxes imposed on natural resources was calculated on the same basis and varied from 25 to 65 percent, depending on the region.

constitution, adopted in 1993, strengthened the role of the federal government and signified the preservation of the state despite these strong centrifugal tendencies.[6]

Although none of these outcomes are surprising or limited to Russia only, they significantly influenced the form of the federalist structure that was to emerge in Russia—a structure that could best be described as asymmetric federalism.[7] Many other studies have reached a similar conclusion, including World Bank (1996). Dolinskaya (2001), Martinez-Vazquez and Boex (2001), and Martinez-Vazquez (2002). Some authors have even questioned whether Russia could be regarded as a federation, given the extent of centralization of its tax regime (Bird, Ebel, and Wallich 1995). During the federation's early days, however, policy makers probably did not grasp the potential risks associated with the implementation of intergovernmental reforms in a country with such vast differences in resource endowments or the implications for macroeconomic stability (Martinez-Vazquez and Boex 2001).

The major thrust for the devolution of some powers to subnational governments during the early period may have derived from the federal government's willingness to come to some sort of compromise. Part of the reason for this willingness came from an increasing awareness that many of the rights that federal government bodies still held in theory became impossible to be enforced in practice because the laws and decrees issued in Moscow were often ignored in the regions (Shleifer and Treisman 2000). The vast distance between the capital city and the region, in some cases well over 9,000 kilometers, as is the case between Moscow and the Far East, and the time difference (as great as 10 hours) further exacerbated any possibility of maintaining regular and speedy interactions.

In the midst of these challenges, a number of developments reinforced emerging democratic institutions. The election of the heads of executive bodies at the subnational government level was a major step toward the establishment of democratic rule. Regions refused to toe the line largely

---

6 For instance, the constitution guaranteed the central bank's independence from interference by both the parliament and the president, while at the same time it gave the president the right to nominate the bank's chair (subject to confirmation by the State Duma) and to recommend the chair's dismissal. Subsequently, the 1995 Law on the Central Bank of the Russian Federation declared that the bank would be both independent from and accountable to the State Duma.

7 Many countries, such as Belgium, Canada, India, and Spain, have implemented asymmetric decentralization of powers to better address existing regional, ethnic, and linguistic diversities (Stepan 1999).

because of the federal government's inability to provide subnational governments with sufficient resources to provide basic services. This situation led to widespread suspicion that the federal authorities were corrupt and that fraud and abuse of power were rampant. The situation remained largely unchanged until 1999, and the deepening of Russia's financial crisis in 1998 could be attributed to the existing nature of the relationship between the federal government and the subjects of the federation.

Although not all regions wielded the same power, those that could exert themselves did so, even withholding their remittances to the federal government. During this period of "interregnum," even weak subnational governments were allowed some leeway, such as issuing municipal bonds without any federal oversight. Indeed, the entire municipal bond market developed free from any such oversight, and early attempts by the federal Ministry of Finance to impose some regulation by denying tax-exempt status to all subnational bonds were retracted.[8] Requests for such exemptions were later handled on a case-by-case basis (Alam, Titov, and Petersen 2004). The outcome of the first stage of reforms (1991–93) was that the central government devolved many of its powers to the regions, and according to some observers, this policy saved the country from total disintegration (Wallich 1994).

Formalization of the Rules, 1994–98

The next stage in the IGFR reform (1994–98) saw the appearance of a new legislative framework for taxation when the Tax Code was passed into law in 1998.[9] In 1994, regional and local governments were granted increased revenue-raising powers by presidential decree. Subnational governments were allowed to introduce new regional and local taxes and to change the rate of profits tax in their jurisdictions. The sharing rates for federal shared taxes, which were uniform for most regions except Bashkortostan, Tatarstan, and Yakutia, were fixed for five years. To equalize regional fiscal capacities, which until that time had been achieved

---

8 Most other developing and transition countries also lack effective regulatory regimes governing local government finances. Only Hungary and South Africa have regulatory frameworks to deal with local government bankruptcy (Shah 2004).

9 Some authors, such as Martinez-Vazquez and Boex (2001), divide the period 1994–98 into two: 1994–96 and 1997–98. However, after close examination of the changes in the legislative framework during this period, we conclude that making such a division is not crucial.

through the use of differentiated sharing rates, the federal government set up an equalization fund, called the Federal Fund for Financial Support of Regions (FFSR), and allocated equalization grants to recipient regions according to a single formula.

The formula for the fund had two equalization windows. The first window was used to distribute funds to regions that had budget revenues that were lower than the country average (needy regions). The second window was used to support regions that had budget revenues that were inadequate to cover the region's expenditure (very needy regions). The formula was based on the principle of gap filling, which was used in the subventions during 1992–93 and dated back to the Soviet era (Gaidar 1996).

At the beginning, the fund was modest, and equalization grants were allocated on the basis of estimated revenues and expenditure needs (the so-called minimum budget). Naturally, regional authorities and the federal government had quite different views on what the regions' revenues and expenditure needs were. The data on actual revenue collection and expenditure failed to measure fiscal capacity of the regions and their expenditure needs. A lack of incentives on the part of subnational authorities to cut back on expenditures and to increase their tax collection efforts resulted in inefficient subnational spending and undercollection of taxes. In addition, the newly granted expenditure powers were not supported by adequate financial resources; as a result, subnational governments started to accumulate debts. Because the regions had no incentives for cutting their spending and wanted to retain employment, they spent a considerable portion of public funds on subsidizing state-owned enterprises that operated at a loss.

In fact, no real estimates of potential taxes and expenditure needs were available until 1999. The problems related to transfers were further compounded by regular adjustments of the formula and intense lobbying activities carried out by some regions during the period leading up to parliamentary discussion of the Federal Budget Law (Jarocińska 2008).[10] In

10 The political factors that determined the transfers apparently changed over time. In the early 1990s, for instance, the regions that received favorable treatment were those that did not support the Yeltsin regime. During the latter part of the 1990s, the political dynamics seem to have changed such that favorable treatment in terms of more federal transfers went to those regions that supported the regime during both the 1995 parliamentary election and the presidential election that was held a year later (Popov 2004; Treisman 1996). A recent analysis also confirms, albeit indirectly, that from 1995 to 1998 the amount of federal transfers received by a region barely correlates with its having a politically powerful incumbent governor. Previously incumbent governors

addition to these transfers under the FFSR, other types of transfers were used from 1995 to 2001—the largest category being *mutual settlements*, an umbrella category that included using transfers in place of financing regional investment programs from the federal budget—to compensate regional governments for carrying out federal government mandates as well as to provide emergency aid.

Novgorod Oblast is a good illustration of the way in which equalization transfers were allocated. Its progressive governor, Mikhail Prussak, offered tax privileges to attract foreign investors. Because the oblast's estimated revenues were low, it received a transfer from the Federal Fund for Financial Support of Regions, which in practice compensated the oblast for its tax exemptions. At the same time, the oblast achieved its goal of attracting foreign investment and its gross regional product increased, but it did so at the expense of regions that received fewer transfers from the federal government.

The weakness of the budget-planning mechanism in the 1990s gave way to the provision of supplementary transfers in addition to those approved by the federal Budget Law. These transfers were allocated in accordance with decisions made solely by the federal Ministry of Finance. They were intended to make up for increases in regional expenditures imposed by the federal government (mandates) after the federal Budget Law had been adopted. The Ministry of Finance also provided regions with interest-free loans that were to be paid back by an unspecified future date.

In 1995, the Law on General Principles of the Organization of Local Self-Government defined the status of local governments and their relationships with regional authorities. According to this law, territories that (a) owned municipal property, (b) formed and executed local budgets (not just expenditure estimates), and (c) elected both representative and executive local self-government bodies were defined as *municipalities*. Furthermore, the law established a list of "issues of local significance," which was the first attempt to assign expenditure responsibilities to local governments.

In 1997, the Law on Financial Foundations of Local Self-Government established the average shares of federal taxes going to local governments. In addition, the Budget Code, adopted in 1998 and put into effect in

---

were able to use transfers to enhance their chances for reelection, but such possibilities gradually declined as the transfer system became more transparent and objective (Jarocińska 2008).

2000, was particularly important because it regulated spending responsibilities and fiscal powers.

Further Steps in Fiscal Decentralization and Political Recentralization, 1999–2001

The beginning of the next stage of IGFR reform (1999–2001) was marked by the prior approval (in 1998) of the Concept for IGFR Reform for 1999–2001, which was the first medium-term program for reforming the system of intergovernmental fiscal relations. Its ambitious goals included improving the efficiency and effectiveness of the management of subnational public finance, equalizing access to public goods across the regions, and accelerating regional development. Unfortunately, these goals were not fully attained within the program's time frame.

The first important change introduced by the IGFR reform program was a new grant allocation formula. This new formula, which allocated equalization grants across regions, included an adjustment that reflected regions' capacity to raise sufficient taxes to cover the costs of delivering public services in their jurisdiction. The formula guaranteed a certain level of per capita budget revenues to the poorest regions, significantly reduced the gap in per capita budget revenues between wealthy and poor regions, and put an end to individually negotiated transfers for each region. It also stopped the mechanism whereby an increase in a region's own revenues reduced the amount of transfers it received, which until that time remained a major disincentive for regions to raise their own revenues. Another important feature of the new transfer allocation formula was that it permitted regions to estimate their next year's transfers on the basis of statistical indicators.[11]

The second important feature of the IGFR reform program was that it eliminated three major federal mandates: allowances for children, in-kind benefits for those with disabilities, and in-kind benefits for federal government employees. Previously, regional governments had to finance these mandates from their general funds, and the federal government never fully compensated them for these centrally imposed spending obligations. As of 2001, all in-kind benefits for federal employees were converted to additional salary payments and were paid from the federal budget. The federal government also recognized its obligation to provide funding for

---

11 Unfortunately, the approval of a new equalization formula did not safeguard it from being subject to annual modifications.

allowances for families with children and in-kind benefits to persons with disabilities. Both mandates were delegated to regional governments with earmarked funds from the Federal Compensation Fund for their implementation. The amounts of the transfers allocated to each region were calculated uniformly for all regions.

The program also provided for the federal government to allocate other types of grants to the regions. The most important of these grants were transfers for capital improvements to public infrastructure (financed by the Regional Development Fund) and grants to induce regional governments to increase socially important spending (financed by the Social Expenditures Cofinancing Fund). Each of these transfer flows was allocated to regions in accordance with a formula.

The third important feature of the IGFR program was that it established rules for regional governments to follow when conducting their fiscal affairs with municipalities. The federal Ministry of Finance developed these rules, which could not be legally imposed on regional governments; however, the rules were approved by federal government resolution, and their observance was strongly recommended and encouraged.

The major outcome of the 1999–2001 IGFR reform phase was a growing understanding among policy makers that Russia needed a stronger push to establish a genuine system of fiscal federalism and that the system of intergovernmental fiscal relations needed comprehensive improvements. The strengthening of the federal government's position started in 1997–98 and received a new impetus with the election of Vladimir Putin as Russia's president in 2000. As mentioned in an earlier part of this study, Russia was subdivided almost immediately after the elections into seven federal okrugs headed by plenipotentiary presidential envoys. These envoys were responsible for their region's legislation and were to ensure that regional affairs complied with federal laws. The president was granted the right to remove governors of regions from office if their activities violated federal legislation. Later on, the system for electing governors was changed, and instead of being selected by direct vote, governors were appointed by regional legislatures following presidential nomination of the candidate.

Even though the regions had gained significant autonomy by the early 1990s, the system of relations between the federal government and the regions was governed more by informal relations between regional and federal officials than by any formal decrees or other legislative mechanisms. To streamline the division of powers and overcome the growing asymmetry in federal relations, the federal government adopted a fiscal federalism strategy in 2001. The strategy, which covered the period through 2005, was the brainchild of the federal Ministry of Finance and promised discipline, clearly assigned expenditure responsibilities, and revenue sources, as well as the creation of a transparent system of intergovernmental fiscal relations.

Assignment of Power and Local Government Reform, 2002–04

Thus, in 2001, with the adoption of the fiscal federalism strategy, the federal government launched a new round of intergovernmental reforms. The main objectives of these reforms were

- To establish a multitiered system of local self-government
- To clarify and optimize the assignment of expenditure responsibilities across tiers of government and to eliminate unfunded federal (and regional) mandates
- To reassign revenue sources to tiers of government in accordance with their newly reassigned expenditure responsibilities and to set this revenue assignment on a permanent basis
- To establish transparent and fair rules for allocating federal and regional intergovernmental transfers
- To improve public financial management in subnational governments

This new strategy was part of a broader administrative and local self-government reform launched by the federal government.[12]

One of the components of the reform touched on the organization of local self-government. Historically, the local government structure below the regional level was complex in terms of both its overlapping jurisdictions and its composition. Kurlyandskaya, Nikolayenko, and Golovanova (2001) identify the following three categories of regions according to the local government systems that existed before 2006 (for a more detailed description of these categories, see Kurlyandskaya 2001; Martinez-Vazquez, Timofeev, and Boex 2006).

The first category included single-tier local governments in large cities and raions. In this case, subraion towns and villages had neither power to

---

12 Dimitry Kozak, deputy head of the President's Office, headed the commission that was put in charge of developing proposals on the reassignment of government responsibilities and local government reform. The reforms proposed by the commission later came to be known as Kozak's reforms.

formulate and execute budgets nor elected bodies. Large cities and raions enjoyed the fiscal rights established by federal legislation, although regional authorities unilaterally designed their fiscal relations with subregional authorities, including the allocation of intergovernmental transfers and tax sharing.

The second category also included single-tier local bodies of self-government in the regions so that regional governments had to deal with only a single set of local governments, including large cities, towns, and villages or rural councils. In this category, regional governments dealt with towns and rural councils through the deconcentrated tier of regional governments located in the raions, which were not elected bodies. The authority to set local taxes was not vested in these raion-level territorial branches of regional administrations. The budgets of raions were part of the regional budgets presented in the form of expenditure plans; thus, raions did not have certain rights and powers that were established for municipalities by federal legislation.

The third category included a two-tier local government structure in which large cities and raions formed the first tier, and subraion towns and rural councils formed the second tier. Both levels were elected by local residents, but only local governments in the first tier were authorized to deal directly with regional governments on financial matters. As a result, no direct relationship existed between the regions and the second-tier local governments in relation to intergovernmental transfers and tax sharing. Local governments of the first tier were responsible for distributing grants to localities of the second tier and for allocating the sharing rates of regional and federal taxes assigned to the local levels by the regional administrations. In effect, the first-tier local bodies often carried out the functions assigned to the regional governments even though the first-tier local governments were not deconcentrated units of regional governments but were local bodies elected by local residents. As Kurlyandskaya, Nikolayenko, and Golovanova (2001) note, these categories led to different combinations of local government administrations in different regions.

A source of major confusion was that before 2005, budget and tax legislation and laws on local self-government assumed that local governments were similar to each other. Consequently, local governments were assigned a common list of local taxes and spending items, ignoring the existence of different types of local jurisdictions and local budgets. Thus, the various powers and revenue and expenditure autonomy that were assigned to one type of local government were rarely suitable for others. Local governments that sprang up largely because of political preferences on the part of regional administrations turned out to be so different that the same legislative rules could not be applied across the board. These entities had vastly different populations and patterns of population dispersal, geographies, ownership of social infrastructure, and so on. The legislation's failure to take these disparities into account led to serious challenges, including the mismatches between (a) the size of a territory over which a municipality had jurisdiction and the powers and competencies assigned to a local government under the law; (b) a fragmented and unevenly distributed revenue base of local governments, which prevented them from responding effectively to demands for public services; and (c) local governments' managerial capacities and the responsibilities assigned to them.

Unfortunately, instead of putting the existing system of local government on a firm legal footing, the legislation passed by the federal government instituted a uniform scheme of organization of local self-government, creating a two-tier model in all subjects of the federation. This system was clearly not going to work given the numerous disparities between regions noted earlier.

The second version of the Law on General Principles of the Organization of Local Self-Government, which was adopted in 2003 and in force since 2006, established local self-governments as one of the tiers of subnational government across the whole country. Thus, the country was divided into cities (*gorodskoi okrugs*) and municipal raions. Urban and rural settlements form the second tier of local government. Regional laws established the boundaries of municipal entities in compliance with the requirements set out in the federal legislation.

The Law on General Principles of the Organization of Local Self-Government established three lists of issues of local importance: one for municipal settlements, one for municipal raions, and one for cities. At the same time, the Budget Code set up three lists of taxes for each type of local government.

The reform of expenditure assignment was aimed at clarifying and reassigning responsibilities falling under the joint jurisdiction of the federation and subjects of federation as established in the constitution—namely, social policy, education, health care, culture, protection of the environment, and response to emergency situations. The federal government believed that having different levels of government share such responsibilities hindered the provision of public services and hampered its control over regional authorities. At the same time, the major problem in intergovernmental relations from regions' and localities' perspective was the lack of funding for expenditures assigned to them under federal laws (unfunded mandates). The federal legislation that regulated public spending was notorious for the following shortcomings:

- Unjustified centralization of the establishment of all norms and regulations
- Unclear assignment of responsibilities for the provision of public goods
- Unclear assignment of responsibilities for funding expenditure obligations, with responsibilities for funding driven by property assignment rather than by government function (that is, the obligation to perform a function became secondary to the obligation to provide adequate spending to a public institution that was assigned to a specific government body)
- Ambiguous and contradictory legislative provisions

In addition, irrational and excessive expenditure obligations set by the federal legislation were a heavy burden for all tiers of government.

Despite the formal assignment of responsibilities by the federal legislation, before 2005 not a single function could be fully assigned to the regional or local level of government. From that perspective, no explicitly federal or regional functions existed. The assignment of spending responsibilities between the federal government and subnational governments replicated the allocation of responsibilities to service delivery institutions, which could belong to any level of government. Rather than assigning functions, the policy that existed before 2005 required that subnational governments provide adequate funding to all service delivery institutions that they had on their books, regardless of their service profile. During the course of reform, policy makers agreed to distinguish between three types of spending responsibilities related to service delivery: (a) setting standards for public service delivery, (b) providing adequate funding to deliver services meeting the required standards, and (c) delivering the actual services. From 2005 onward, the setting of standards for the delivery of public services and the responsibility for providing adequate funding for such services must remain at the same level of government (whether federal, regional, or municipal). The delivery of services may be transferred to a lower level of government only if the commensurate funding is provided in the form of special-purpose (or strictly conditional) grants or transfers.

The reform was supported by two basic laws passed earlier: the Law on General Principles of the Organization of Government in Subjects of the Federation and the Law on General Principles of the Organization of Local Self-Government. For the reform to be workable, however, the federal government had to amend 152 federal laws regulating particular aspects of the provision of public goods and to repeal 41 federal laws. The amendments to the legislation required that funding be provided in cases where one level of government imposed spending obligations on another level of government, thereby abolishing unfunded mandates. Appropriate amendments were introduced into the Budget Code and Tax Code to further reinforce the reforms.

To align each government's expenditure responsibilities with its revenue-raising capacity, amendments to the legislation discontinued inefficient expenditure obligations, such as the provision of benefits to pharmacy employees, and unrequested entitlements, such as the provision of subsidies to book collectors. The logic behind the reform was that the federal government should stop regulating how regions executed the powers assigned to them. However, the passage of laws that reduced the federal government's social obligations within the regions was extremely unpopular among regional leaders.

To some extent, the elimination of unfunded mandates was achieved by providing funding for them. To provide adequate funding for the mandates, which from 2005 were referred to as federal functions delegated to the regional level and which consisted mostly of payments to war veterans and victims of the Chernobyl disaster, the federal government reduced the regions' shares of federal taxes and then transferred those revenues back to the regions as special-purpose transfers. These special-purpose transfers were provided to every regional government, whether it was wealthy or poor.

Another way of eliminating unfunded federal mandates was by limiting federal regulation. Since 2005, the federal government can only establish a framework for regulation concerning matters of regional competence, while regional laws are to set detailed standards. Because the constitution does not permit reducing the amount or quality of public services, regional governments do not have a completely free hand in setting their own standards for the functions transferred to them from the federal government. As a consequence, the regions found that they could neither abolish social benefits that the federal government had transferred to them nor reduce the level of financing.

To clarify the assignment of functions, the reform included a division of property between regions and localities. Because federal laws no longer entitle regions or municipalities to own property that is not related to the execution of powers assigned to them, municipalities were ordered to transfer property not directly related to the performance of their local functions to regional governments, and regions had to transfer property to be used to perform municipal functions back to municipalities. These transfers were to be effected without any compensation for the loss of assets. Many municipalities started selling off (privatizing) their property, including buildings occupied by bodies of the regional administration. The courts were swamped with actions brought by regions against municipalities and by municipalities against regions. As a result of this and other problems, the new law on local self-government was suspended, and the enactment of some of its provisions was postponed until 2009.

Using the new proposals for expenditure assignments, the federal Ministry of Finance estimated the changes in spending obligations of each level of government and proposed a new assignment of revenue sources and new sharing rates for federal taxes. The proposed assignment of revenue sources was eventually set in the Tax Code and the new sharing rates were set in the Budget Code. Before the reform, the sharing rates could change every year, because they were approved annually as part of the federal budget law. By setting fixed rates in the Budget Code, the federal government made the distribution permanent. The new assignment of revenue sources across tiers of government was guided by international best practices and took into account such considerations as stability of revenue flow, economic efficiency, mobility of the tax base, and evenness of the distribution of the tax base across jurisdictions.

Unfortunately, the assignment of greater responsibilities to regional authorities in relation to social policy issues was not accompanied by greater taxing powers. A primary focus on the interests of the business community and of taxpayers and on the progressive goals of making the tax system simpler and tax administration easier meant that tax reforms disregarded the federative nature of the country, whereby each level of government should enjoy true autonomy over revenue determination and management. Nevertheless, setting fixed tax rates was a step toward having a more stable and a transparent revenue assignment system compared with the previous system. Because of these reforms, the share of subnational expenditures remained unchanged (see figure 3.1), while the share of subnational revenues shrank (figure 3.2) from 55 percent, at its highest in 1998, to about 34 percent in 2006.

The 2002–05 Program of Fiscal Federalism Development did not propose any significant modifications to the grant allocation formula

Figure 3.2   Share of Subnational Revenues in Total Revenues of National and Subnational Government without Extrabudgetary Funds, 1992–2006

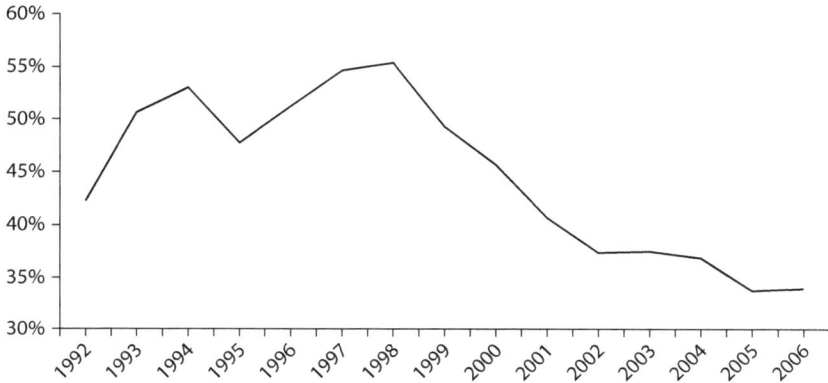

Source: Authors' calculations based on Ministry of Finance data (excluding extrabudgetary funds).

introduced in 2001, but in the pursuit of perfection, the formula was subject to annual modifications. The rules for computing the two main grant allocation parameters—estimates of regional tax capacity and estimates of regional expenditure needs—changed every year, hence preventing the regions from making medium-term projections of their revenues.

The 2004 amendments to the Budget Code established common rules for allocating equalization grants to regions and localities and limited the number of different types of intergovernmental grants allocated to regions, which included equalization grants, matching grants, and grants to compensate for federal mandates. To secure the fiscal independence of the two tiers of municipal government, the amendments required the regions to provide direct transfers to both tiers. These amendments came into force as of fiscal 2006, although regions were allowed to introduce them gradually during a transition period until 2009. Thus, the major outcomes of the reform were to clarify and reassign expenditure areas for which the federal government and the regions were jointly responsible, eliminate unfunded mandates, and reduce excessive expenditure obligations. In addition, equalization transfers to the regions are now based on a formula that has been incorporated into the Budget Code rather than determined on the basis of negotiations between the central and regional governments.

Fiscal Recentralization, 2005–08

Like the previous stages, this stage was accompanied by an official federal program—in this case, the Concept for Increasing the Efficiency of Intergovernmental Relations and Improving Subnational Finance Management in 2006–08. Unlike previous programs and strategies pertaining to intergovernmental relations, this program, which was devised by the federal Ministry of Finance in 2006, does not propose any radical changes. Its major objectives are to maintain the existing state of affairs, adapt intergovernmental fiscal relations to the medium-term budget framework, and ensure that regional and local governments follow the new federal regulations on intergovernmental relations and subnational finance management.

According to the official text, the program has the following goals:

- Strengthening regional fiscal autonomy
- Encouraging regional and municipal governments to increase their revenue efforts
- Encouraging regional and local governments to improve their public finance management
- Increasing the transparency of regional and municipal financial operations
- Providing regional and municipal governments with technical assistance in arears of intergovernmental fiscal relations and public financial management

Unfortunately, the steps included in the action plan that accompanied the program were aimed mostly at strengthening federal control mechanisms and maintaining the design of the newly established system of intergovernmental fiscal relations. Thus, concrete government actions to strengthen the fiscal autonomy of subnational governments are still lacking.

The program calls for stability in relation to federal tax legislation and federal regulations concerning the allocation of intergovernmental transfers. To achieve this goal, the program requires the three-year budget of the federal government to specify the amounts of equalization transfers due to each region three years ahead of time. This step is important in providing stability to the regions and moves away from the pattern of previous years, when the tax laws regulating both federal and subnational taxes were amended almost every year. The program does not propose any other steps to move subnational governments closer to fiscal autonomy. During the program period, the federal government does not intend to grant subnational governments the right to introduce their own taxes or piggyback their taxes on federal ones, nor does the federal government intend to share its tax administration authority with subnational governments.

The most visible incentive for subnational governments to increase their revenue efforts is the federal sanctions for low tax capacity and high expenditure needs (table 3.2). These sanctions are, however, unlikely to improve the financial performance of poor regions, because they have weak tax bases and low tax autonomy to begin with. The latest edition of the Budget Code also provided for similar sanctions against poor financial performance by local governments (table 3.3).

Another program measure aimed at encouraging regional growth was the amendment of the transfer allocation formula to benefit regions that demonstrated higher-than-average economic growth. The program also proposed giving rewards to regions and municipalities that made the biggest progress in their public finance management practices. A formal procedure was proposed to monitor the quality of public financial management across regions.

Table 3.2   Sanctions for Poor Financial Performance by Regional Governments

Share of federal grants in total revenues of a regional government	Sanctions
0 ≤ 20%, 46 regions in 2006	None[a]
20% for two consecutive reporting years 33 regions in 2006	• The salary of regional officials or total wage expenditures shall not exceed the ceiling established by the federal government. • The regional government shall follow the federal Ministry of Finance's on eliminating payment arrears.
> 60% for two consecutive reporting years 7 regions in 2006	• The regional governments must reduce the budget deficit and government debt. • Regional spending is limited to matters explicitly listed as regional expenditure responsibilities in federal legislation. • The regional government shall sign an agreement with the federal Ministry of Finance to increase the efficiency of regional spending and enhance collections. • The federal government audits-end of-year regional budget execution reports.

Source: Authors, based on the Concept for Increasing the Efficiency of Intergovernmental Relations and Improving Subnational Finance Management in 2006–2008 and the Budget Code (version of January 1, 2008).
a. For the general limits on the size of debt and debt service set by the Budget Code.

Table 3.3   Sanctions for Poor Financial Performance by Local Governments

Share of grants (including tax transfers) in total revenues of a local government	Sanctions
0 ≤ 10%	None[a]
> 10% for two consecutive reporting years	Salary of local officials shall not exceed the ceilings established by the regional council.
> 30% for two consecutive reporting years	Local spending is limited to matters explicitly listed as local expenditure responsibilities in federal and regional legislation.
> 70% for two consecutive reporting years	• The local government shall sign an agreement with the regional government to increase the efficiency of local spending and enhance collections. • The local government's budget is submitted to the regional government for approval. • The regional government audits-end of-year local budget execution reports at least every other year.

Source: Authors, based on the Budget Code (version of January 1, 2008)
a. For the general limits on the size of debt and debt service set by the Budget Code.

CHAPTER 4

Intergovernmental Design

In recent years, Russia's intergovernmental design has changed dramatically as a result of reforms. Formally, federal, regional, and municipal governments have separate responsibilities and powers. Each level of government formulates and approves its own budget without the approval of the higher-level government, and each has its own designated revenue sources and responsibilities. However, the fiscal autonomy of regions and municipalities is narrowly constrained: the total spending of regional and municipal governments depends on higher-level decisions. Subnational governments cannot estimate the total amount of revenues available to them in the next fiscal year.

Thus, rather than having genuine autonomy in relation to fiscal choices, most subnational governments find themselves financially dependent on the federal government. Regional governments cannot levy any taxes other than those established by the Tax Code or other federal laws. The system of revenue assignment is such that almost all taxing powers are concentrated at the federal level, and federal laws determine the primary distribution of revenue sources between regions and municipalities. Each level of government is assigned retention rates of shared federal taxes, and tax sources are labeled as regional or local, although the tax base and the range within which the rates of those taxes can vary are set by the federal government.[1]

Expenditure Assignment

Federal laws lay down those functions that fall within the jurisdiction of subnational governments. The 1993 constitution lists the exclusive responsibilities of the federal government as well as the joint responsibilities of the federal government and the subjects of the federation.[2] The list of joint responsibilities contains broad governmental functions, such as education, health care, and social welfare, without a further breakdown into primary, secondary, and higher education or into first aid, ambulatory services, primary health care, and specialized health care. The Law on General Principles of the Organization of Government in Subjects of the Federation clarifies these joint responsibilities.

In assigning expenditure responsibilities across different levels of government, the law divides education and health care by categories, which are assigned across levels of government according to principles of subsidiarity, economies of scale, and spillover effects (externalities).[3] For instance, higher education was assigned to the federal government; vocational education to the regions; and primary, secondary, and preschool education to the local governments. Expenditure responsibilities for tasks such as controlling pollution, protecting forests and water facilities, and responding to natural disasters were assigned according to the scale of spillover effects. In the case of culture, objects of cultural heritage rather than functions were divided between the federal government and the regions. Each government level is

---

1 These developments have led some authors to conclude that an important element of fiscal federalism—namely the revenue discretion of subnational governments—is absent in Russia (Thiessen 2005).

2 Some rationale exists for having joint responsibilities. Take the case of primary education or primary health care services. Local governments are likely to provide these services more effectively, given the size of benefit areas. At the same time, these services have important implications for overall welfare and income distribution, which is often the responsibility of the central government. Therefore, as some scholars point out, the notion of a best assignment of expenditure responsibilities is not meaningful and may even change over time because of varying costs, technological developments, and so on. However, establishing clear, concrete expenditure assignments at any given time is necessary, and failure to do so will likely cause instability in intergovernmental relations and inefficient provision of public services (Bird and Vaillancourt 2006).

3 See Shah (1994) for one possible way of assigning expenditure responsibilities between different levels of government.

responsible for the safety and legal regulation of those objects of culture assigned to it. In the housing and utilities sector, the framework for housing relations is governed by the federal Housing Code, while tariffs for electricity are established by regional energy committees, and local authorities set the tariffs for other communal services (such as domestic solid waste disposal). The federal government, however, sets the average tariff level and for some time has set the maximum annual tariff growth indexes.

In the field of social protection, the responsibility for legal regulation is split between the federal government and the regions. The federal government is responsible for veterans and radiation victims, while the regions are responsible for workers in defense enterprises during World War II, victims of Stalin's regime, families with children, and low-income individuals. The regions have the discretion to establish the amount of entitlements or compensation for those groups for which they are responsible.

The assignment of responsibilities for social protection of individuals became a source of serious conflict. During reforms to monetize social benefits that used to be provided as in-kind benefits, the federal Ministry of Finance grossly underestimated the costs of providing the monetary grants to replace the in-kind benefits for those beneficiaries who fell under the jurisdiction of the federal government and regional governments. Moreover, the federal government mandated that regional governments should provide welfare support to certain categories of former federal beneficiaries without providing the regions with adequate funds to implement this mandate. These categories included workers in defense enterprises during World War II, whereas World War II veterans were covered under the federal budget.

The federal government also transferred the responsibility for providing free public transportation to old-age pensioners to the regions, which led to a great deal of resentment not only among regional government officials, but also among the recipients of the benefits, because the monetary compensation they now received did not cover the full cost of transportation. In January 2005, old-age pensioners in Moscow and nearby cities, deeply resentful of the loss of their right to use public transportation services free of charge, demonstrated along highways. This action soon led to an agreement signed by the governments of Moscow and Moscow region whereby each agreed to recognize the rights of pensioners and other groups of eligible individuals to free (or subsidized) use of public transportation. In 2005, the federal government took advantage of its budget's record-breaking surplus to substantially increase the amount of transfers to regions to help address some of these needs.

Even though the reform was aimed at enhancing regional expenditure autonomy, legal control over and regulation of almost all key matters are still in the hands of the federal government. The regions are allowed to establish their own legislation and regulations on matters that are their direct responsibilities, as long as such laws and regulations do not conflict with federal laws and regulations and are not detrimental to citizens in general or to certain groups of recipients of public services. Social policy thus became the responsibility of regional authorities, but the federal government did not grant them greater taxing powers. As a result, regional authorities became more accountable to higher levels of government than to the citizens whom they served.

The new assignment of functions between the federal government and the regions became effective at the beginning of 2005, and the list of local issues has been in force since the beginning of 2006. In 2005 and 2006, several amendments were made in the assignment of powers to the federal government and regions. For the most part, these changes were based on what regions had volunteered to assume; therefore, no funds from the federal budget were provided to support them, except in relation to registration of civil status and conscription. Box 4.1 lists the main regional government functions.

Box 4.1

The Main Functions Assigned to Regional Governments

The main functions assigned to regional governments are as follows:

- Providing health care in specialized hospitals (for tuberculosis, cancer, psychiatric conditions, and so on)
- Providing funds to municipalities for preschool, primary, secondary, and after-school education
- Providing vocational education
- Protecting the environment and nature reserves
- Preventing disasters and emergencies and dealing with their aftermath
- Providing fire protection
- Providing veterinary clinics
- Providing welfare services to senior citizens and persons with disabilities
- Paying allowances to families with children and to low-income households (for housing and utilities)

(continued)

Box 4.1 *(Continued)*

- Supporting victims of Stalin's regime and workers in defense enterprises during World War II
- Providing medical insurance for the unemployed
- Running orphanages
- Preventing terrorism
- Constructing and maintaining regional roads and other infrastructure
- Providing intercity public transportation
- Maintaining regional public libraries and regional museums
- Organizing cultural and sports events

Having abandoned asymmetrical federative relations with the republics (their privileges had been abolished in the course of intergovernmental reform), the federal government has created a new source of asymmetry by considerably curtailing the powers of autonomous okrugs.[4] In autonomous okrugs, the main social functions over which regions have jurisdiction, such as education, health care, fire protection, welfare services, and social allowances, are exercised by the government of the oblast or krai that includes the specific autonomous okrug. Accordingly, federal tax revenues assigned to the regional level and collected in the territory of an autonomous okrug go to the respective oblast or krai budget unless a different procedure is established by means of an interregional agreement. For some regions, this kind of asymmetry was yet another argument for a merger, whereas other regions have signed supplementary agreements on the assignment of expenditure responsibilities and revenues.

The list of local government functions is determined by the Law on General Principles of the Organization of Local Self-Government. In the case of settlements, local issues include functions whose regulation could be fully assigned to the lowest level of public administration (box 4.2).

---

4 During the Soviet period, autonomous okrugs were parts of the larger regions (oblasts, krais). They had some autonomy, but were not equal in rights to oblasts, krais, or republics. In the 1990s, autonomous okrugs were recognized as subjects of the federation, and the 1993 constitution confirmed the equality of all subjects of the federation in their relations with the federal government. However, as a result of the reforms in assignment of power, the powers of the autonomous okrugs were curtailed compared with those of other types of regions.

Box 4.2

Local Government Issues

The main functions assigned to municipal raions are the following:

- Providing preschool, primary, and secondary education along with supplementary after-class education, using subsidies from the regional budget
- Providing health care in general hospitals, maternity care, and ambulance services
- Providing municipal police (however, having localities provide this service would require amending the existing law enforcement system; therefore, implementation of this particular item has been postponed until 2010)
- Protecting the environment
- Managing waste disposal
- Maintaining raion libraries
- Organizing recreational, cultural, and sports events
- Providing electricity and gas
- Constructing and maintaining intersettlement roads
- Providing intersettlement public transportation

The main functions assigned to settlements are the following:

- Delivering housing and utilities (electricity, heating, water, gas, streetlights) and providing waste collection
- Constructing and maintaining housing for low-income households
- Providing basic fire protection
- Maintaining cemeteries
- Maintaining parks and gardens
- Maintaining settlement libraries
- Organizing recreational, cultural, and sports events and recreational activities for teenagers
- Constructing and maintaining intrasettlement roads
- Providing intrasettlement public transportation

The scope and performance of these functions are determined largely by the preferences of settlement inhabitants. These functions do not include providing health care or education; in those areas, therefore, citizens are protected from the risk of declining budget revenues. Nevertheless, subraion municipalities are assigned such tasks as providing housing, including that for low-income individuals, and providing utilities. The performance of these functions requires not only much larger revenues for local budgets, but also a highly skilled group of municipal employees. Furthermore, failure to properly perform the functions may pose a serious threat to balancing local budgets. Local government issues assigned to cities include those related to both municipal settlements and municipal raions (box 4.2).

Regions and localities are free to add more functions to the federal list of functions only if they have their own resources to support them, but recipients of equalization transfers are not allowed to perform any functions other than those established by federal law. The federal government has the right to unilaterally assign certain federal government functions to regions and localities, together with the financial and material resources to support them, and it makes substantial use of this right. Table 4.1 provides a general idea of the current assignment of responsibilities across different levels of government; however, the figures reported in table 4.1

Table 4.1   Expenditures on Public Functions by Tier of Government as a Percentage of Total Expenditure, 2006

Government function	Federal budget (%)	Regional budgets (%)	Local budgets (%)
Total outlays	54	29	17
General public services	64	20	16
Public administration	9	21	70
Courts	89	11	0
Fiscal authorities	86	8	5
Elections and referenda	42	45	13
International affairs	97	3	0
Research and development	99	1	0
Debt service	85	13	3
Defense	100	0	0
National security and law enforcement	77	20	3
Police	62	33	5
Penitentiary system	100	0	0
Disaster protection and emergencies	67	24	9
Fire protection	33	62	5
National economy	36	56	8
Fuel end energy	41	39	20
Agriculture and fishing	24	71	6

(continued)

Table 4.1   Expenditures on Public Functions by Tier of Government as a Percentage of Total Expenditure, 2006 *(Continued)*

Government function	Federal budget (%)	Regional budgets (%)	Local budgets (%)
Forestry	77	22	1
Transport	32	59	9
Communication	30	67	3
Housing and utilities	8	49	43
Environmental protection	29	57	15
Education	22	26	52
Preschool	1	16	82
Primary and secondary	1	21	78
Vocational	28	69	2
Retraining and continuous	53	44	3
Higher professional	95	5	0
Culture, cinematography, and mass media support	29	39	32
Health care and sports	22	59	19
Health care	13	69	18
Sports and physical fitness	13	58	29
Social welfare	81	14	5
Pensions	100	0	0

Source: Authors' calculations based on the Ministry of Finance consolidated government budget and consolidated regional budget 12-month execution reports as of January 1, 2007 (extrabudgetary funds are included).

do not always provide an accurate picture. For instance, social benefits—for which funds from the federal budget are received but for which the actual services are provided by regional social institutions—are reported under federal budget expenditures as intergovernmental transfers rather than as spending on social welfare.

Even though the authors of Russia's intergovernmental fiscal reforms claim that the assignment of expenditure responsibilities was based on standard principles of subsidiarity, economies of scale, and spillover effects, in some instances the actual assignment of responsibilities is not always consistent with the subsidiarity rule. One of the key elements of any responsibility—its legal regulation—is almost fully governed by federal laws. Even if one assumes that the scope of responsibilities is measured by the scope of expenditures, the subsidiarity principle is adhered to only with respect to education. The share of local spending is also high in relation to expenditures on housing and utilities, while the share of regional governments on these is even higher. As table 4.1 shows, regions rather than localities provide much of what should traditionally be local services (for example, fire prevention and police protection).

Local branches of federal authorities (deconcentrated units) also perform many regional and local functions. The courts at all levels, public prosecutors' offices, police departments, tax authorities, and statistical agencies are all federal entities. The justification given is that these functions belong to the central government because they involve enforcement, and under the constitution, local governments are not bodies of state power. Thus, local bodies have neither the right to pass laws nor the power to enforce them. In a few cities, such as Moscow, St. Petersburg, Perm, and Saratov, municipal police departments were established, but they followed orders of the federal Ministry of the Interior rather than those of the local administration. Local authorities' involvement in this area boiled down to simply financing and maintaining municipal police stations.

Expenditure autonomy

One of the most important constraints on subnational expenditure autonomy is that subnational governments are responsible for meeting standards and norms established by the federal government. Because regional and local governments are effectively assigned to provide basic social services guaranteed by the constitution, localities also tend to adhere to the same standards prescribed by the federal government, especially in areas such as education and health care. The regional governments make federal norms more specific and establish regional norms and standards in areas not covered by the federal government. For instance, Moscow Oblast has more than 60 spending norms that localities must meet, and compliance with federal and regional standards and norms is ensured by relevant branches of regional administrations.

As noted earlier, federal legislation has prohibited unfunded mandates since 2005, and federal responsibilities delegated to subnational governments are now financed through subventions. An inevitable result of financing mandates through subventions is the concentration of subnational budgetary funds in regional budgets. (The share of earmarked grants in local government revenues now stands at 42 percent.) Education is one of the most resource-intensive responsibilities financed through subventions to local budgets. Subventions designated for purchases of textbooks and technological aids, payment for other school needs, and remuneration for staff are provided to all cities and municipal raions, whether they are wealthy or poor. At the same time, substantial cuts in

Table 4.2   Differences in Regional Expenditures for Major Public Functions Structure, 2006

	Share of outlay per public function in total outlays (%)		
Line item in budget classification	Median	Maximum	Minimum
General public services	8.9	19.2	3.2
National security and law enforcement	4.9	13.8	0.9
National economy	12.2	51.7	3.0
Housing and utilities	10.8	50.9	3.2
Education	26.2	38.0	8.3
Culture, cinematography, and mass media support	3.6	6.1	1.4
Health care and sports	17.3	22.7	3.6
Social welfare	12.6	22.9	1.2

Source: Authors' calculations based on Ministry of Finance consolidated regional budget reports as of January 1, 2007.

the nonearmarked funds available to local governments narrowed their spending choices.[5]

Even though the federal government's regulatory role shrank somewhat as a result of the reform of intergovernmental relations, a large number of federal laws, bylaws, orders, and instructions that regulate government outlays still exist. Nevertheless, decisions on public spending are not 100 percent centralized. The differences in expenditure composition across subjects of the federation, as shown in table 4.2, demonstrate that subnational governments can still choose some spending priorities on their own, even though this freedom is far more limited for local governments than it is for regional governments.

As table 4.2 shows, regional governments spend from 8.3 to 38.0 percent of their budgets on education, while the share spent on housing and utilities varies from 3.2 to 50.9 percent. The regions differ significantly in the extent of subsidies they provide to different sectors of the economy, such as industry, energy, construction, agriculture, fisheries, and transportation. A closer examination of budget execution reports demonstrates that regional priorities account for a significant portion of

---

5 One pitfall that the federal government should avoid is to increase transfers without reciprocal reductions in spending at the federal level. A number of Latin American countries (such as Colombia and Mexico) fell into this trap, causing significant fiscal deficits (Burki, Perry, and Dillinger 1999).

subnational budgets, which suggests that fiscal decentralization reforms have had some positive effect in terms of delegating expenditure responsibilities to lower levels of government. Another indication of the degree of subnational autonomy is provided in figure 4.1, which shows how per student spending on secondary education differs from region to region.

In recent years, however, the federal government has attempted to curtail regional governments' spending powers through amendments to the Budget Code. Thus, those regions where federal financial support for two consecutive reporting years exceeded 20 percent of budget revenues (not including earmarked transfers) have no right to establish and execute expenditure responsibilities other than those explicitly assigned to them by the constitution and federal laws (see table 3.2). They also may not exceed the remuneration and operating cost standards established by the federal government for federal civil servants. In addition, the Federal Audit Chamber, which is responsible for financial audits, or the Federal Service for Fiscal Control audits the annual budget execution reports of those subjects of the federation whose share of federal transfers has exceeded 60 percent of their budget revenues for two consecutive years.

Figure 4.1   Annual Expenditures per Student on Secondary Education, by Region, 2005

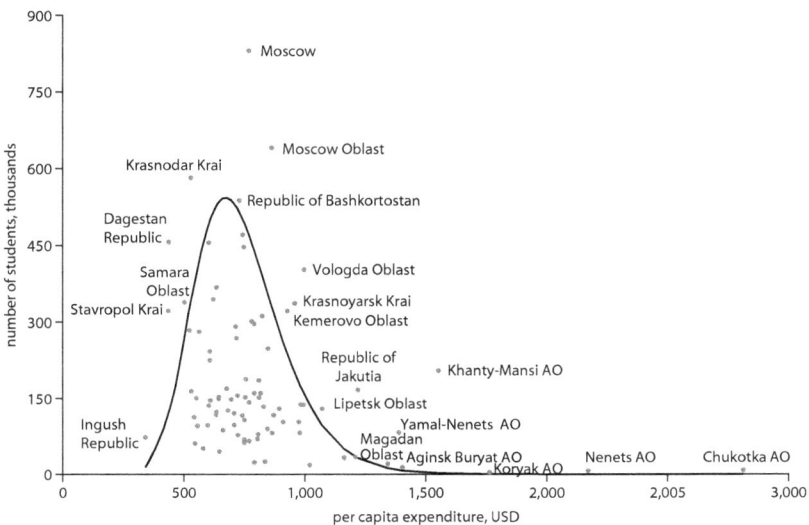

Source: Authors' calculations based on the Ministry of Finance consolidated regional budget reports as of January 1, 2006, adjusted for the cost of fixed product and services baskets (Rosstat).
Note: AO = Autonomous Okrug.

Similar powers were conferred on regional financial control bodies to deal with local governments (see table 3.3). The aim of these controls is to see whether the actual spending is in accordance with the list of functions established by federal laws.

The 2003 Law on General Principles of the Organization of Local Self-Government provides a set of controls for local governments that fail to execute their main responsibilities that is more stringent than those established in any previous legislation. The regional administrations may temporarily assume the powers of local governments when the lives, health, and safety of residents are threatened; during natural calamities or other emergency situations; when the overdue debt of municipalities exceeds 30 percent of their budget revenues (not including earmarked transfers); or when budgetary funds are spent for purposes for which they are not intended or in violation of federal legislation. These controls come into effect at the slightest failure of municipalities' responsibilities.

If a local government subject to sanctions fails to live up to its obligations under its agreement with the regional government or exceeds its budget deficit or borrowing ceiling, then the regional government can cut back on or withhold intergovernmental grants (except earmarked grants) to the defaulting local government until that local government corrects the situation. However, poor financial performance by local governments is not always entirely their fault. They are only partially responsible because higher levels of government are responsible for the revenue-sharing and expenditure assignments.[6]

Assignment of Revenue Sources

In all countries, expenditures are more heavily decentralized than revenues (Ebel and Yilmaz 2002). The decentralization of expenditures—which should always precede the decentralization of taxing powers for well-known reasons[7]—permits decentralizing service provision to suit

---

6 According to the Federal Audit Chamber, only about 2 percent of cities are financially self-sustainable.

7 There is an underlying logic for starting with the expenditure assignment because expenditure responsibilities assigned to different levels of government will require different forms of financing. For instance, local public utilities could be financed by user charges while some other services with externalities—such as health, education, or environmental services—might require financing that involves other levels of government (regional or central). For a more detailed description, see Bahl and Linn (1992).

local preferences, which is especially important for a country as vast as Russia. However, the decentralization of taxing powers gives rise to transfer pricing, tax competition among jurisdictions, and other negative consequences. In contrast, the centralization of taxing powers confers certain advantages—for example, removing companies' incentives to avoid taxes by registering in jurisdictions with lower tax levels while actually operating in jurisdictions with higher tax levels. Centralization also makes tax collection simpler and more cost-effective.

A weakness of a system with decentralized expenditure responsibilities and centralized taxing powers, however, is that it provides subnational governments with perverse incentives to increase spending while relaxing their tax efforts, thereby making such governments even more dependent on transfers from the central government. Therefore, granting subnational governments the full revenue autonomy is also fraught with risks, as the recent experiences of Argentina and Brazil indicate. The regions were under pressure from their constituents to spend more while taxing less (Dillinger and Webb 1999). The perverse incentives provided by the implicit guarantee of an eventual bailout of them and their creditors by the central government allowed the regions to continue these policies until their fiscal deficits became unsustainably large.

The perennial question, then, is how much tax autonomy for subnational government is desirable. A distinction should be made between the types of tax autonomy that could be granted to subnational government, which could include the autonomy to define the rate, the base, or both. Clearly, autonomy to change tax rate is more desirable than the other two alternatives, although all of them will have far-reaching implications on interjurisdictional fiscal competition, horizontal imbalance, and so forth (Martinez-Vazquez 2007).

In the literature on this issue, two criteria have been mentioned that provide some guidance to solving the taxing problem. The first is to allow subnational governments to raise their own revenues *at the margin*. The second is to manage these resources under hard budget constraints, which implies that revenue sharing and grants from higher levels of government will be used only for *inframarginal funding*.[8] Still the problem of assessing the sufficient tax autonomy at the margin remains, largely

---

8 Subnational fiscal autonomy requires not only that subnational governments have their own sources of revenue, but that they be able to control the level of revenue at the margin (that is, to be able to set the level of taxes that corresponds to the desires of voters). The argument that revenue sharing and grants should represent only *inframarginal*

because expenditure needs and their regular changes are hard to quantify. Furthermore, it is also difficult to know in advance the extent to which the central government is able and willing to reduce the horizontal imbalance (an outcome of tax autonomy). Some argue that one way to overcome this challenge is to measure the expenditure needs of the subnational governments more frequently so that information is up to date. In addition, it may be possible to set an upper limit ("golden rule") by allowing the tax revenues not to exceed the amount required (net of conditional grants) to cover expenditure needs of the wealthiest subnational governments (Martinez-Vazquez 2007).

Until 1991, the tax system in Russia was heavily centralized. Each region, city, and raion was assigned its own revenue sources, supplemented with grants transferred from the central government, but these amounts were not their primary source of revenue, especially for localities. Regional governments received payments from the profits of enterprises falling under their jurisdiction, a share of payments from the profits of enterprises falling within the jurisdiction of central government ministries and agencies, state duties, revenues from movies shown within their territories, and small amounts from local taxes and duties. Local governments received only a share of the profits of local enterprises. As a consequence, subnational authorities did not have a tax culture—that is, an understanding that all economic agents should share their revenues with all levels of public administration at preestablished rates and that relevant government bodies should establish such rates to determine what shares of revenue would be accrued where, depending on the demand for public services.

Russia's transition to a market economy led to major changes in the tax system, but those changes were applied only to taxpayers, not to the recipients of taxes. The federal government constrains subnational governments' revenue options, and federal legislation has established a list of regional and local taxes. It also mandates the tax base to be used for particular taxes and the rates of those taxes. Currently, neither regional nor local governments have the power to levy taxes other than those established by federal legislation, although between 1994

funding is quite simple: if the purpose of revenue sharing (or grants) is only to provide subnational governments with funds and not to alter their decisions in other ways, they should be inframarginal. In that case, subnational governments should be required to exercise little or no independent fiscal effort to receive funds from revenue sharing, because revenue sharing is generally not a source of marginal own funds. The only fiscal autonomy that is granted in such a case is to allow subnational governments to make their own decisions on how to spend the money (McLure 1998).

and 1996, a presidential decree gave them the authority to do so. The federal government discontinued this practice when regional and local governments failed to compensate for the revenue losses that the federal government sustained due to the introduction of local taxes. These taxes threatened interregional trade and increased the total tax burden.[9] In addition, the administrative costs of collecting many small local taxes exceeded the amounts collected. Now the federal government has the discretion to unilaterally levy or cancel regional or local taxes, change tax rates, and grant tax breaks.

Currently, Russia has 15 main taxes (many of which are just a grouping of smaller taxes based on certain characteristics) that consist of 10 federal taxes (including the special tax regimes for certain types of businesses), 3 regional taxes, and 2 local taxes (table 4.3).

Federal tax revenues assigned to the regional level and taxes collected in autonomous okrugs go to the respective oblast or krai budget unless a special interregional agreement is in effect. Local governments of cities enjoy the combined taxing powers of urban and rural settlements and municipal raions. The revenue sources of municipalities located within the borders of the city districts of Moscow and St. Petersburg are established by the laws of the respective subjects of the federation as these two federal cities have the status of subjects of the federation.

Excise taxes on alcohol and alcohol-based products and on gasoline and diesel fuel are redistributed among the regions on a formula basis. Formally, federal legislation establishes the tax base for all taxes, but subnational governments can grant tax exemptions with respect to their "own" taxes. In addition, for the single tax on imputed income, raions or cities can select activities to be taxed from the federal list and set an adjusting coefficient (ranging from 0.005 to 1.0) applicable to the tax base, as determined by the Tax Code. The regional tax rate for profits tax is 17.5 percent, which regions can reduce to 13.5 percent.

Because the federal government decides the base of the subnational governments' "own" taxes thus, providing no room for tax autonomy (except to allow exceptions and set an adjusting coefficient), it is clear that the benefit principle has not been used in determining these taxes. The benefit principle requires that a clear link be established between the benefits received by residents and the local taxes and spending. In

---

9 For instance, Buryat Republic levied a so-called octroi tax on goods imported from other regions.

Table 4.3   Tax Assignment for Various Levels of Government, 2006

Tax	Base	Rate	Federal	Regional	Municipal raions	Settlements
Federal taxes						
Enterprise profit tax	F	F	27	73		
Value added tax	F	F	100			
Personal income tax	F	F		70	20	10
Excise taxes						
On alcohol and alcohol-based products	F	F	50	50		
On gasoline and diesel fuel	F	F	40	60		
On alcoholic products, beer	F	F		100		
Other	F	F	100			
Mineral resource extraction tax						
Gas	F	F	100			
Hydrocarbons other than gas	F	F	95	5		
Common minerals	F	F		100		
Other minerals	F	F	40	60		
Fee for the use of aquatic biological resources	F	F	100			
Fee for the use of fauna	F	F		100		
Water tax	F	F	100			
Single social tax	F	F	100			
Special federal tax regimes						
Single tax on imputed income	L(F)	F	10		90	
Single tax levied under an applicable simplified taxation system for small businesses	F	F	10	90		
Single tax on agricultural enterprises	F	F	10	30	30	30
Regional taxes						
Enterprise property tax	F	R		100		
Transport tax	F	R		100		
Tax on gambling businesses	F	R		100		
Local taxes						
Personal property tax	F	L				100
Land tax	F	L				100

Source: Tax Code and Budget Code.
F = federal, R = regional, L = local governments.

other words, efficient resource allocations require that people pay for the public services they demand and receive—and more so if the quality of the services they receive is satisfactory. It should become clear to the residents that tax revenues are used to improve the services that they demand and consume. Therefore, the benefit principle implies that residents will not make excessive demands for services, because they will have to pay for them. The advantages of benefit taxes also imply that revenue assignment problems are inextricably linked to the expenditure assignment problem (Bird 2000; McLure 1998).[10]

The Russian taxpayers pay taxes to governments at all levels, through the branches of the Federal Treasury. The Federal Tax Service exercises oversight to ensure the accuracy of these payments. Neither regions nor localities have their own tax authorities or the power to administer tax collection. Furthermore, regional and local authorities have no right to enter into contracts on a chargeable basis with federal tax bodies on levying local taxes. As a rule, federal tax offices are not particularly effective at collecting taxes that accrue 100 percent to regional or local budgets; thus, the collection rate is much lower for local and regional taxes than for federal taxes. However, in the case of shared taxes and enterprise profit tax (for which the federal government and the regions set their own rates on the same tax base), the collection rate is high for the federal portion of revenues, and these taxes also go toward regional budgets. The reason for the difference in collection rates is that until 2005 the tax authorities had collection targets for taxes that accrued to the federal budget but no collection targets for subnational taxes.

Lacking the legal rights to administer and collect taxes, subnational governments use administrative pressure on taxpayers (especially on legal entities), such as publishing the names of entities that fail to pay their share, initiating audits of various kinds, and providing information about delinquent taxpayers to federal tax authorities and the public prosecutor's office. In many cases, conflicts related to tax payments between businesses and local governments have paralyzed companies' operations and have eventually culminated in the sale of the companies for the purpose of paying back taxes. Hence regional and local authorities often succeed in getting even large taxpayers to pay their taxes the hard way, but they could also provide incentives to law-abiding taxpayers by providing

---

10 The relationship between taxes and benefits is often weak and, therefore, limits the literal application of the benefit theory of taxation. However, the theory can guide decisions on tax assignment. For instance, if the "generalized benefits" of public services—benefits that cannot be financed by fees, charges, and taxes closely related to benefits—are more closely related to where people live than to where they work, a consumption-based sales tax or a residence-based income tax would be preferable to a production-based sales tax or a source-based income tax. Moreover, tax harmonization, which may be needed to simplify compliance and administration, should not extend to the choice of tax rates (McLure 1998).

Figure 4.2   Consolidated Tax Revenue Structure

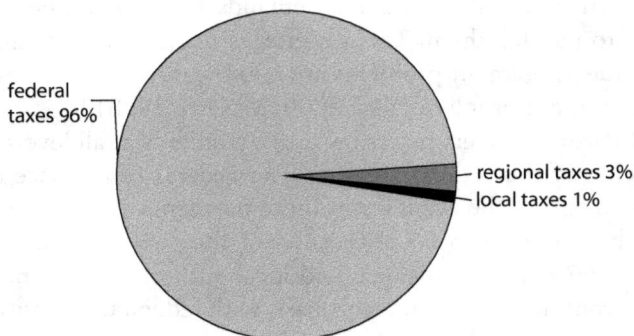

federal
taxes 96%

regional taxes 3%
local taxes 1%

Source: Authors' calculations based on the Ministry of Finance consolidated budget reports as of January 1, 2007.

tax breaks, budget loans, or budget guarantees for commercial loans or by allocating land for lease or sale to taxpayers.

On average, regional taxes account for 3 percent of total budgetary tax collections and local taxes account for 1 percent, with federal taxes accounting for the remaining 96 percent (figure 4.2). Regional and local taxes represent 11 percent of subnational governments' tax revenues (8 percent of total subnational revenues). Federal shared taxes account for the biggest share of subnational revenues. Most regions and municipalities levy taxes at the maximum rate allowed; for example, only 13 regions reduce the rate of enterprise profits tax for selected groups of taxpayers. However, tax exemptions are used widely. The options for regional and municipal bodies to increase their revenues include leasing regional and municipal property and engaging in entrepreneurial activity, which, according to some official sources, currently accounts for about 10 percent of their total revenues.

Revenue autonomy

Regional and local autonomy to raise revenues relates to regional and local governments' rights to grant exemptions from taxes and to establish the rates of certain taxes (within ranges established by the federal government). For example, even though the full amount of personal income tax accrues to subnational budgets, it is nevertheless a federal tax, and the central government sets both the base and the rate. Subnational governments are allowed only to grant deductions from the taxable base, and even then they can grant only those deductions that are listed in the Tax Code.

Until recently, regional governments could decide to reduce the regional rate of the enterprise profits tax to zero. Some regions, such as Chukotka, Kalmykia, and Mordovia, used this opportunity to set themselves up as domestic offshore zones. These regions gained from increased collections of other taxes that taxpayers registered in their jurisdiction had to pay and from registration fees. Presumably, the offshore regions received additional benefits from informal agreements with taxpayers seeking to avoid taxes. Rather than attracting actual businesses to the regions, however, this strategy simply contributed to growth in the number of head offices registered in these regions for tax-avoidance purposes.

The lack of fiscal powers makes regions and localities seek alternative ways to generate revenues, such as levying fees to issue various permits, selling land, or constructing and selling buildings. Regions and localities tend not to report their income from entrepreneurial activities in their budgets, because doing so is not in their interests. The disclosure of additional revenue sources may lead the federal government (or regions, in the case of localities) to reduce the amount of transfers allocated to them as most regions and municipalities receive financial aid (Alexeev and Kurlyandskaya 2003; Zhuravskaya 2000). Furthermore, a higher level of government may confiscate revenue-generating assets from the lower level by claiming, for instance, that holding property is inconsistent with the functions of local authorities and that such property should, therefore, either be sold to the private sector or be transferred to the higher level of government.

To assess the degree of tax autonomy of subnational governments, this study uses the classification of tax powers developed by the Organisation for Economic Co-operation and Development (OECD 1999). According to this classification, taxes are subdivided into the following categories, ranked in order of decreasing control that subnational levels of government can exercise over the revenue source:

a. Subnational governments set tax rate and tax base.
b. Subnational governments set tax rate only.
c. Subnational governments set tax base only.
d. Tax-sharing arrangements are in place:
   d.1 The subnational governments determine the revenue split.
   d.2 The revenue split can be changed only with the consent of subnational governments.
   d.3 The central government can unilaterally change the revenue split fixed by legislation.

d.4 The higher-level government determines the revenue split as part of the annual budget process.

e. Central government sets tax rate and base.

In cases *a* through *d.2*, subnational governments have significant control over tax revenues. In the remaining cases, their tax autonomy is limited or nonexistent.

Table 4.4 assesses the tax autonomy of subnational governments in Russia and selected other countries in accordance with this classification. Russian subnational governments have limited freedom to set rates, and there are federal limits on maximum rates (table 4.4). Nevertheless, this study assigns such taxes (regional and local taxes and enterprise profits taxes) to category *b*. For the single tax on imputed income, raions and cities select taxable activities from the federal list and, as noted earlier, can impose an adjusting coefficient to the tax base as defined in the Tax Code. Although this ability could be seen as a measure of autonomy in relation to the tax base, this tax is shared according to the rate established in the Budget Code. Therefore, this tax is classified as one of category *d.3*. Even though all tax decisions by the federal government are enacted following the approval by the Federation Council—in other words, all amendments to tax revenue allocations to the various tiers of government are formally agreed upon with subjects of the federation—in practice, the Federation Council has little or no influence on the federal government's tax policy. The cancellation of important regional taxes—such as the sales tax—illustrates the council's weakness. For this reason, shared taxes are included in the *d.3* category and not in the *d.2* category.

Table 4.4 shows that even though Russian subnational governments have a higher share of tax revenues than subnational governments in the other federations, the Russian local governments are considerably less autonomous than those in the other countries. Sixty percent of the tax revenues of a region come from the regional piggyback part of the enterprise profits tax and regional taxes. In the case of local governments, only 10 percent of tax revenues come from local taxes: on average, 75 percent of local tax revenues come from taxes assigned to localities by the Budget Code, and an additional 15 percent are shared in accordance with regional legislation, which changes more often than federal legislation. Since the 2005 intergovernmental reforms, however, tax assignments for subnational budgets have become more stable. The share of local taxes in local tax revenues was halved, but a sizable amount of tax revenues is now

Table 4.4 Subnational Tax Revenues by Degree of Tax Autonomy, Selected Countries

Subnational government tax revenues in consolidated budget	Type of subnational tax autonomy according to the OECD classification							
	a	b	c	d.1	d.2	d.3	d.4	e
Austria **18**								
Local governments 8	9	11			81			
Bundesländer 10	2				98			
Germany **29**								
Local governments 7	1	52			47			
Bundesländer 22					100			
Mexico **20**								
Local governments 4						74		
States 16	14				86			26
Spain **14**								
Local governments 9	33	51			16			
Autonomous communities 5	15	7			78			
Switzerland **38**								
Local governments 16	16	97				3		
Cantons 22	89				6	5		
Russian Federation **46**								
Local governments 8		10				75	15	
Regions 38		60				40		

Source: OECD Tax Policy Studies, Taxing Powers of State and Local Government, 1999; data for the Russian Federation were calculated on the basis of the regional and local budget 12-month execution reports as of January 1, 2007.

a. Subnational governments set tax rate and tax base.

b. Subnational governments set tax rate only.

c. Subnational governments set tax base only.

d. Tax-sharing arrangements are in place:

d.1 The subnational governments determine the revenue split.

d.2 The revenue split can be changed only with the consent of subnational governments.

d.3 The central government can unilaterally change the revenue split fixed by legislation.

d.4 The higher-level government determines the revenue split as part of the annual budget process.

e. Central government sets tax rate and base.

established by federal legislation instead of being determined by annual regional budget laws, so local revenues have become more predictable.

To assess the degree of autonomy of subnational governments, table 4.5 shows the share of own subnational revenues in the composition of total revenues. Regional own revenues amount to 51 percent of total regional government revenues, which means that about half of total revenues available to regional governments come from transfers and shared taxes. Own revenues are not truly "own," however, because the federal government establishes tax benefits and privileges (for example, property tax), and most importantly, introduces and cancels regional and local taxes.[11] Revenue-raising capacity varies significantly across regions. When one looks at the consolidated budget, subnational governments may seem to have financial autonomy, even though regional budgets incorporate a relatively insignificant share of own revenues and only a few regions are relatively independent of the federal government.

Table 4.5   Subnational Government Revenue Structure, 2006

Revenue category	Share in total budget revenues (%)	
	Regional government	Local government
Own revenues	**51.3**	**15.6**
Own tax revenues,[a] which include	42.9	3.6
Enterprise profit tax	34.8	×
Regional taxes	7.9	×
Local taxes	0.1	3.0
Own nontax revenues (including entrepreneurial activity)	8.4	12.6
Shared revenues	**38.1**	**42.5**
Shared taxes,[b] which include	29.0	27.0
Personal income tax	20.2	18.8
Shared nontax revenues	0.4	0.3
General-purpose transfers	8.8	15.1
Earmarked transfers	**10.6**	**41.9**
Total	**100.0**	**100.0**

Source: Calculated from regional and local budget 12-month execution reports as of January 1, 2007.
Note: Extrabudgetary funds are not included.
a. These are the taxes of categories a–c in table 4.4.
b. These are the taxes of categories d–e in table 4.4.

---

11 The decision to cancel taxes is always both unilateral and unexpected. Counter to best practice in taxation, the federal government canceled the local housing and utilities tax (a turnover tax). In 2004, to reduce the tax burden, it also abolished the regional sales tax, which the regions had been made to impose.

Local governments rely heavily on funding from higher-level authorities, while their own revenues account for only 16 percent of their budgets, whereas shared revenues and earmarked transfers account for roughly 42 percent each. Such a low level of revenue autonomy makes local governments in Russia extremely weak compared with those in some other countries (for example, China) that have a history of relatively more recent decentralization reforms (see box 4.3).

Box 4.3

Local Government Revenue in China

The outcome in Russia is starkly different from the experience of local governments in China, where they have played a significant role in the country's growth. Devolution of powers to subnational governments and the assignment of expenditure and revenue responsibilities have led to a phenomenon that some observers call *local government corporatism* (Nee and Su 1996). The entrepreneurial roles taken by local leaders since the 1980s have had a distinct effect on economic growth, and the transfer of some state-owned enterprises to local government has led to growth at subnational levels (García 2008; Zhu 2004). One clear example of the positive role played by local governments is the significant contribution of town and village enterprises during the first decade of reforms (Che and Qian 1998).

Local governments receive a disproportionate share of revenues because of a system of fiscal contracts (a "fiscally responsible" system) that was put in place in 1988 between the central government and local governments and later codified in the 1994 Budget Law. Although the 1994 reforms did not give local governments the autonomy to set their tax rates or to change the bases of collection, the contracts stipulated a lump-sum remittance (a subsidy) of the profits of enterprises accrued to each province. These contracts also allowed an annual increase at an agreeable rate, with any additional revenues going directly to the provinces. In return, the provinces were granted the authority (budget authorization) to cover their expenditure requirements from the share of revenues accrued to them. As some scholars point out, this new tax-sharing system led to a fundamental change in China's fiscal system by delinking revenue sharing from expenditure needs, thereby setting local governments on a path of self-financing for the first time (Wong and Bird 2005).

(continued)

Box 4.3 *(Continued)*

In addition, a significant amount of extrabudgetary funds (EBFs) were available at the subnational levels. These EBFs pay for expenditures such as social safety nets (pensions, unemployment insurance, disability, minimum income support, and so forth) and capital investment (especially investment in infrastructure in need of repair or replacement). Virtually all levels of government—even down to the municipal districts and villages—are able to extract payments under the guise of different fees from local businesses and residents. Hence, the bulk of China's EBFs remain at the subnational level, which holds almost absolute control and discretionary power over them. The proliferation of fees and charges by local governments has, caused the local population a considerable degree of hardship and, as some authors have noted, "has the potential to cause serious social unrest and political difficulties for the center" (Ahmad, Singh, and Fortune 2004). However, there are serious distortions and inefficiencies in resource allocation and public service provision, because local governments are often pressed to set priorities that have little relation to local needs (thus violating the benefit principle).

As mentioned earlier, during the 1990s, tax reforms were neither complex nor coherent and dealt only with individual components of the system. The first significant step took place in 1994, when all regional governments were granted equal taxing powers and were assigned federal taxes at equal sharing rates. The allocation of tax powers was aimed at achieving vertical balance of the budgetary system. The search for the optimal vertical balance went on for 10 years; the federal government kept changing the regions' sharing rates year after year, and often a change in the sharing rate of one tax necessitated changes in the sharing rates of other taxes.

Thus, the decision for the federal government to retain 100 percent of the value added tax as of 2001 was well founded, both from the theoretical and the practical points of view, because the VAT has an uneven tax base, is concentrated in the wealthiest regions, and cannot be distributed in proportion to the value added produced in the regions.[12]

---

12 McLure (1994b) pointed out almost a decade earlier that both Russia and Ukraine made a serious mistake—similar to the one Brazil made a quarter-century ago—by assigning revenues from the VAT to the state level. Although subnational governments in these two countries did not impose a VAT, revenues from the VAT imposed by the central government were shared with lower levels of government.

However, as a result of this reassignment, the regions were deprived of revenues on which they had relied. During 2001–05, the regional share of the tax on extraction of oil and gas resources was cut from 60 percent to 5 percent for oil and to zero for gas. Consequently, the revenues of Tyumen Oblast and other wealthy regions shrank unexpectedly without any compensation for the loss. This measure was good in terms of achieving equalization, given the uneven tax base; however, the federal government should have used the tax revenue to equalize regional fiscal capacities. Only in 2005 did the Budget Code fix the shares of federal taxes that the regional governments would retain (figure 4.3).

Even though regions have virtually no fiscal powers and hence cannot pursue an independent fiscal policy, they can and do compete for taxpayers. The main tax competition instruments available to the regions are tax cuts and tax exemptions. As noted earlier, before 2004, at least three domestic offshore zones—Chukotka, Kalmykia, and Mordovia—used a low enterprise profits tax rate for businesses registered in their jurisdictions. As of January 1, 2004, regions could reduce the 24 percent rate of the enterprise profits tax by only 4 percentage points, but many

Figure 4.3   Sharing Rates of Main Taxes Shared with Subjects of the Federation, 1992–2007

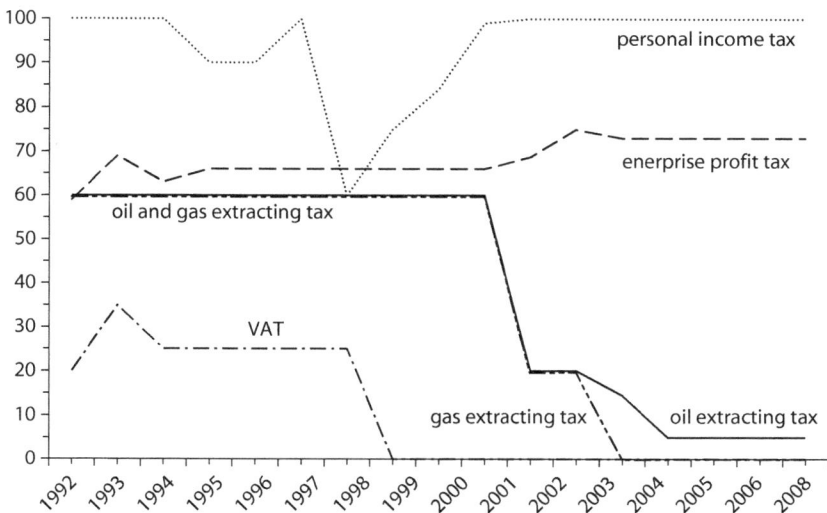

Source: Federal budget laws, 1992–2007.

subjects of the federation did so to attract taxpayers from other regions, as happened in 2005 when Perm Oblast launched a wide-ranging public relations campaign to attract taxpayers by establishing the regional enterprise profits tax rate at 20 percent.

As of early 2008, tax competition has not triggered the collapse of any region, but the competition has been increasingly tough, with 2005 marked by a few notorious cases that could potentially ruin entire regions. For instance, one of Russia's largest oil-producing companies, Sibneft, whose U.K.-based billionaire owner, Roman Abramovich, was elected as the governor of Chukotka Autonomous Okrug, until recently paid a share of its taxes to Chukotka. Sibneft had registered its branch responsible for supplying crude oil to foreign markets, Sibneft-Chukotka, in Chukotka. In 2005, Sibneft was acquired by Gazprom, a state-owned company that refused to pay taxes to the Chukotka region. Although the exact amount of taxes Sibneft paid to Chukotka has not been officially reported, it presumably accounted for a substantial share of Chukotka's budget, which in 2004 was about US$640 million, a quadrupling since 2001, when Abramovich was elected governor. Sibneft's new owners, Gazprom, decided to change the company's place of registration to St. Petersburg, where Sibneft's new headquarters are now located, thereby depriving Chukotka Autonomous Okrug of a substantial amount of tax revenue.

Transfers from the Federal Budget

The Budget Code, which regulates the allocation of transfers to regional and local governments, includes principles of equalization for the allocation of transfers, principles of compensation for federal mandates and budget loans, and eligibility conditions. Existing tax revenue assignments and regional disparities hinder the achievement of vertical balance, and the imbalance becomes worse over time, as can be inferred from the widening gap between the share of subnational revenues and the share of subnational spending. These gaps are now filled by means of intergovernmental transfers (figure 4.4); financial gaps are no longer filled by adjusting the sharing rates. Just before the recent financial crisis, the federal government's total annual spending on financial aid to the regions was equivalent to about 12 to 14 percent of its expenditures, and in 2004–06, this financial aid covered about 16 percent of subnational governments' expenditures. These financial aid flows to regional budgets come in the form of earmarked and general-purpose grants. Box 4.4 shows the different types of transfers.

Figure 4.4   Vertical Fiscal Balance

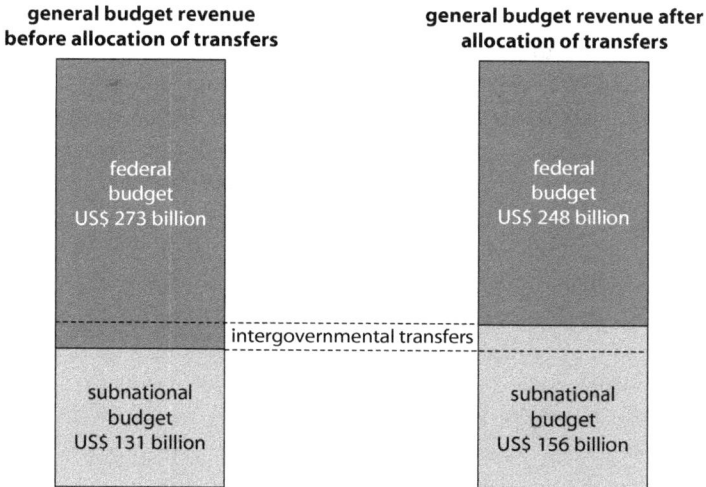

| general budget revenue before allocation of transfers | general budget revenue after allocation of transfers |

```
┌─────────────────┐          ┌─────────────────┐
│                 │          │                 │
│    federal      │          │    federal      │
│    budget       │          │    budget       │
│  US$ 273 billion│          │  US$ 248 billion│
│                 │          │                 │
│- - - - - - - - -│intergovernmental transfers│- - - - - │
│   subnational   │          │   subnational   │
│    budget       │          │    budget       │
│  US$ 131 billion│          │  US$ 156 billion│
└─────────────────┘          └─────────────────┘
```

Source: Twelve-month execution budget reports as of January 1, 2007 (extrabudgetary funds included).

Box 4.4

Types of Federal Transfers

Equalization grants: Allocated through a formula, these general-purpose grants in 2006 amounted to US$8.7 billion. The Budget Code used to impose restrictions on these grants, which could be spent only on so-called protected expenditure items, mostly wages, if regions owed outstanding liabilities in wage payments. This restriction effectively turned equalization grants into wage subsidies, and regional finance officials referred to them as such. Those restrictions have now been canceled.

Gap-filling subsidies: First introduced in 2004, these subsidies compensate regions for losses of tax revenues or increased expenditure burdens that result from federal policies. In 2004, for example, these funds were allocated to the regions to cover their losses from wage increases mandated by the federal government. In 2005, these subsidies served three purposes: (a) to partially cover the regions' losses from changes in the allocation formula for equalization grants; (b) to compensate the regions for changes in federal tax legislation, namely, the federal government's higher retention rates of the oil and gas extraction tax, the 100 percent retention of the water tax, and the 1.5 percent increase in the retention rate of the profits tax; and (c) to cover additional spending responsibilities (for example, for vocational

(continued)

Box 4.4 *(Continued)*

schools) assigned to subnational governments. The 2005 and 2006 allocation formulas did not include compensation for wage increases in 2004, and the 2006 allocation formula did not include compensation for the 2005 tax and expenditure assignment changes. In 2006, the total subsidies equaled US$1.9 billion.

Compensation for federal mandates: The federal government compensates subnational governments for 100 percent of their expenditures on federal government responsibilities. In 2006, the amount paid totaled US$2.8 billion. Fully covered federal mandates include the subsidized rent entitlements granted to certain categories of federal beneficiaries, such as war veterans or victims of radiation catastrophes; the benefits paid to blood donors; and the costs of running civil registration offices. This type of transfer is not financial aid but rather a special mechanism that allows the federal government to perform its own functions at the subnational level.

Cofinancing of social expenditure grants: Partial compensation was provided for certain regional social expenditures totaling US$994 million in 2006. Most of these expenditures were established by federal laws before reforms of expenditure assignments and could therefore be treated as federal mandates. In 2005, the relevant federal laws were abolished, and regions had to introduce their own laws pertaining to allowances to families with children and support to victims of the Stalin regime and workers in defense enterprises during World War II.

Capital transfers: These amounts include capital transfers under federally targeted programs and capital investments not related to such programs are further subdivided into regional development programs—that is, federal programs whose beneficiaries are individual regions or groups of regions and nationwide programs such as education or the expansion of information technology.

Subnational finance reform grants: These grants are awarded to the regions and municipalities that have submitted the best plans for reforming their public finance management systems and that have successfully implemented those plans. In 2006, these grants totaled US$55 million. The World Bank initiated this reform program in 2000, and it is considered one of the most efficient federal grants.

Operating transfers to special territories: These transfers cover subsidies to Chechnya and to irradiated localities.

Ad hoc subsidies: Examples include the annual Best-Run City Award (US$3 million), the 2006 grant to Krasnoyarsk Krai (US$76 million), and the 2007 grant to Koryak Autonomous Okrug.

Transfers to restricted-access cities: These transfers are direct general-purpose subsidies to centers of the defense industry and research and development.

As can be inferred from the names of the transfers listed in box 4.4, most of them are earmarked, although the biggest—equalization grants (see figure 4.5)—and gap-filling subsidies are general-purpose transfers. The grants for cofinancing social expenditures resemble matching grants where the federal government estimates the regions' expenditure needs for certain social expenditures and provides transfers to the regions to cover a fixed share of those needs. These grants, however, perform no incentive functions. Increased regional spending on entitlements or services triggers no obligations for the federal government to increase its portion of funding. The 2007 amendments to the Budget Code consolidated all cofinancing grants, including cofinancing of social expenditure grants, subnational finance reform grants, grants for financing national projects, and other current expenditure transfers in the Fund for Cofinancing of Expenditures.

The federal government has no policy documents that lay out the goals and objectives of intergovernmental fiscal regulation. The policy in relation to subjects of the federation could be inferred only from actual allocations of intergovernmental transfers. For example, the goal of allocating equalization grants to the regions, which was to attain the minimal assured level of

Figure 4.5   Federal Transfers to Subnational Governments as a Percentage of GDP, 1996–2007

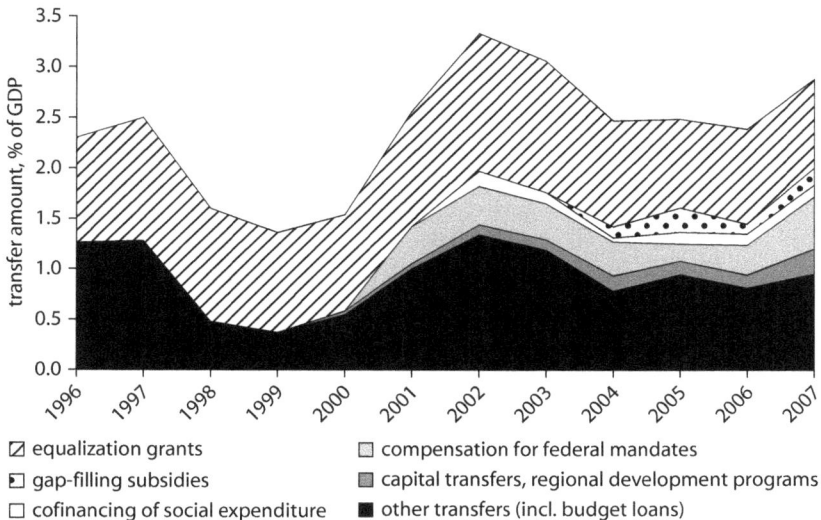

Legend:
- ☑ equalization grants
- ▣ gap-filling subsidies
- ☐ cofinancing of social expenditure
- ☐ compensation for federal mandates
- ▨ capital transfers, regional development programs
- ■ other transfers (incl. budget loans)

Source: Authors' calculations based on federal budget laws and Ministry of Finance budget reports.

assessed fiscal capacity by all subjects of the federation, was not stated explicitly until 2007. Clarity with regard to specific goals and objectives of the grants is further obfuscated by the fact that both the number of funds through which the federal government allocates grants to the regions and the pattern of grant allocation change almost every year.[13]

As a rule, the pool of total intergovernmental grants is determined on the basis of the previous year's figure, with adjustments for changes in budget and tax legislation. Certain types of grants are adjusted for inflation, while others are not and are budgeted on the basis of political considerations. For instance, the 2005 pool for the Federal Fund for Financial Support of Regions was established at the 2004 level, adjusted for expected growth in the consumer price index (1.08),[14] whereas the Best-Run City Award has been equivalent to US$30 million for many years and has not been adjusted for inflation. The 100 percent compensation for federal mandates has been adequate for covering the estimated financing requirements. No formalized methodology is in place for calculating the regions' expenditure needs for maintaining the required balance (gap-filling subsidy), and the total pool of these grants changes from year to year.[15] Nevertheless, in this case, too, the Ministry of Finance presumably takes the previous year's spending into account.

Equalization transfers

In 2005, per capita gross regional product in the richest region was about 69 times higher than that in the poorest region, whereas in 2006, per capita revenue before transfers in the richest region was 151 times that in the poorest region (see appendix A). The richest regions in terms of per capita budget revenues are those that produce oil and gas, while the poorest are the republics of the northern Caucasus, which, because of ethnic strife and religious and other conflicts, have virtually no tax revenues and rely primarily on federal transfers. Contributing to the problem are differences in expenditure needs that arise because regions must deal with different climatic conditions and transportation distances, implying

---

13 One possibility is that the federal government uses new transfers in return for regional compliance with federal initiatives, as, for instance, Argentina did to "achieve a series of fiscal agreements in 1991–94" (Dillinger and Webb 1999: 6).

14 As of 2007, the transfer pool for the Federal Fund for Financial Support of Regions must be large enough to achieve the equalization goal set by the federal government.

15 The methodology for grants allocation for 2004–05 is available at the Ministry of Finance Web page, but it is not open for the last years. The fund also includes an *ad hoc* component.

substantial differences in their energy needs. Thus, the cost of living in one region can be as much as three times higher than that in another region (Federal State Statistics Service 2007). The aim of the equalization transfers to regional budgets is to reduce this gap in per capita revenue between the richest and the poorest regions.

A major part of the equalization grant pool is allocated by means of a sophisticated formula, which limits the possibility for regions to influence the allocation. To measure expenditure needs, the formula uses a set of ratios that are based on statistical data and expert assessment, which adds an element of nontransparency. Nevertheless, the equalization transfers are generally successful in terms of the bulk of such transfers going to those regions that need them.

The formula-based allocation as used in 2001–04 seemed to be transparent and logical (box 4.5). All regions were ranked in ascending order by ratio of the fiscal capacity index to the expenditure needs index. The fiscal capacity index shows potential tax collections compared to the average level of tax collection. Per capita fiscal capacity (per capita revenues before transfers) was estimated based on Federal State Statistics Service data. Regional value added as estimated by the Federal State Statistics Service was used as a tax base in 2001–07 (box 4.6). The fiscal capacity was adjusted for spending needs by means of the index of expenditure needs, which takes a number of factors into account, including nonmarket factors that increase the costs of services to the budget. The relative effect of these factors was estimated on the basis of Federal State Statistics Service data and expert assessments. Finally, 80 percent of the equalization grants were allocated to regions whose per capita fiscal capacity (tax base) was below average, while the remaining 20 percent were distributed among the poorest regions.

In 2005, the allocation principle was changed (see box 4.5). During the first stage, all regions that collected less than 60 percent of average tax collections received transfers that covered 85 percent of the gap. During the second stage, the remainder of the fund was distributed among all regions that collected less-than-average taxes in proportion to the difference between their level of collections and the average level (figure 4.6).

With the transition to multiyear budgeting in 2008, the resulting allocation was fixed for the entire multiyear period (three years). In line with amendments to the Budget Code that took effect in 2008, the size of the equalization fund was determined on the basis of the minimal per capita fiscal capacity requirement that all regions should meet after the allocation of equalization grants. Previously, the size of the fund had

Box 4.5

Allocation of the Equalization Grants

2001–04	2005–10
F is the total amount of the fund (exogenous).	F is the total amount of the fund (exogenous for 2005–06, endogenous for 2008–10).
$K1$, $K2$ are per capita equalization criteria. $K1 = 1.00$; $K2$ is endogenous.	$K1$, $K2$ are per capita equalization criteria. $K1 = 0.60$; $K2 = 1.00$.

2001–04:

$$F_i = T1_i + T2_i$$

$$\sum_i T1_i = 0.80 \times F$$

$$\sum_i T2_i = 0.20 \times F$$

$$T1_i = 0.80 \times F \times \frac{D1_i}{\sum_i D1_i}, \text{ if } D1_i > 0,$$

$$\text{else } T1_i = 0$$

$$D1_i = A \times \left(K1 - \frac{FCI_i}{ENI_i} \right) \times ENI_i \times N_i$$

$$T2_i = D2_i, \text{ if } D2_i > 0,$$

$$\text{else } T2_i = 0$$

$$D2_i = \left(K2 - \frac{A \times FCI_i + T1_i}{ENI_i} \right) \times ENI_i \times N_i$$

F_i is the equalization grant to region i.
$T1_i$ is the first part of the grant for region i.
$T2_i$ is the second part of the grant region i.
A is per capita average tax capacity.
N_i is population.

2005–10:

$$F_i = T1_i + T2_i$$

for 2008–10 after equalization

$$\left[\frac{FCI_i}{ENI_i} + \frac{T1_i + T2_i}{ENI_i \times N_i \times A} \right] \geq$$

$$\geq \underset{\text{without 10 richest and 10 poorest regions}}{\text{average}} \left(\frac{FCI_i}{ENI_i} \right)$$

$$T1_i = 0.85 \times D1_i, \text{ if } D1_i > 0$$

$$\text{else } T1_i = 0$$

$$D1_i = A \times \left(K1 - \frac{FCI_i}{ENI_i} \right) \times ENI_i \times N_i$$

$$T2_i = \left(F - \sum_i T1_i \right) \times \frac{D2_i}{\sum_i D2_i}, \text{ if } D2_i > 0,$$

$$\text{else } T2_i = 0$$

$$D2_i = A \times \left(K2 - \frac{T1_i}{ENI_i \times N_i \times A} + \frac{FCI_i}{ENI_i} \right) \times ENI_i \times N_i$$

FCI_i is the fiscal capacity index, which shows potential tax collections compared with the average level of tax collection.
ENI_i is the index of expenditure needs, which shows relative costs of providing public services compared with the average level.

Source: Ministry of Finance methodologies, adapted by the authors.

Box 4.6

Transfers and Tax Competition

Before 2008, to allocate the pool of equalization grants, the Ministry of Finance derived estimates of regional fiscal capacity from regional value-added estimates provided by the Federal State Statistics Service, which collects information about profits at the point of actual generation of such profits. In contrast, the tax service levies enterprise profits tax at the place of registration of a business. If a business is registered in Chukotka, Kalmykia, or Mordovia, it should, from the tax service's perspective, pay the full amount of tax in that region. Thus, the business pays tax at the lower tax rate granted to it by the regional government where the company is registered but where it may not necessarily have any business units. Because the Ministry of Finance relied on Federal State Statistics Service data, it overestimated the fiscal capacity of regions where businesses' operating units were actually operating. However, because these regions were mostly rich oil producers, they were not eligible for equalization transfers anyway. The appeal of the foregoing tax arrangement for the offshore regions was that they could both receive federal transfers and acquire extrabudgetary revenues or noncash payments from businesses registered in their territories for the "services" the regions rendered.

As a result, in 2002, the Republic of Mordovia granted US$700 million in tax concessions, to enterprises whereas its own capacity to generate revenues from all taxes as estimated by the Ministry of Finance methodology amounted to only US$130 million. At the same time, as a region with low per capita budget revenues, Mordovia received federal equalization transfers and capital transfers for regional development. The size of the tax exemptions granted by Mordovia by far exceeded the amount of transfers it received from the federal budget.

been determined on an *ad hoc* basis. This minimal fiscal capacity level is determined as the average fiscal capacity of all regions except the richest 10 regions and the poorest 10 regions. Another new development is that the formula for estimating fiscal capacity was amended, and a representative tax system estimate was used instead of the estimate based on regional value added.

Other federal transfers

In addition to the formula-based equalization transfers, the federal government uses a number of other options for allocating grants to regional

Figure 4.6   Equalization Grants Allocation Formula, 2005

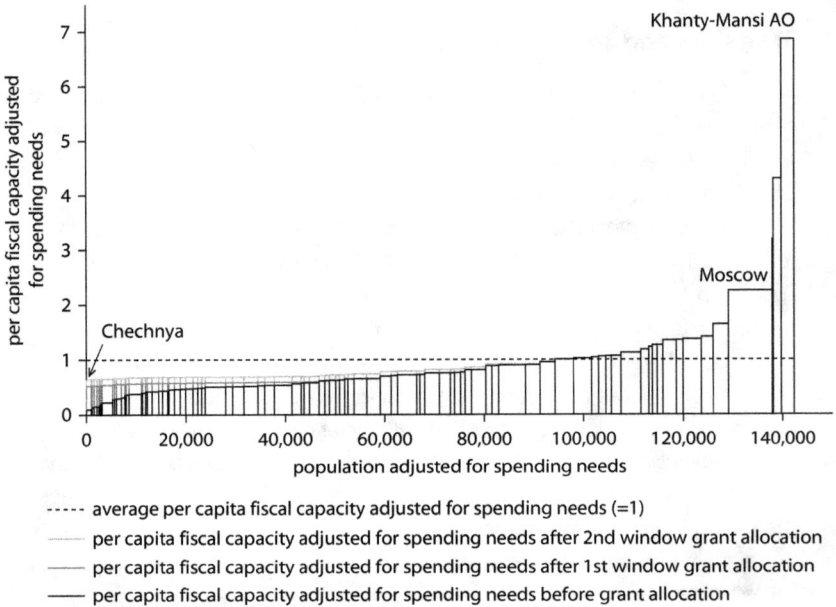

----- average per capita fiscal capacity adjusted for spending needs (=1)
——— per capita fiscal capacity adjusted for spending needs after 2nd window grant allocation
——— per capita fiscal capacity adjusted for spending needs after 1st window grant allocation
——— per capita fiscal capacity adjusted for spending needs before grant allocation

Source: Authors calculations based on Ministry of Finance data.

budgets (see table 4.6). Of the grants reported in table 4.6, equalization grants, part of the gap-filling subsidies, compensation for federal mandates, cofinancing of social expenditures, and a small part of capital transfers—that is, about half the transfers distributed to regions—are based on formulas.

The distribution of grants to participants in the Subnational Finance Reform Program is transparent, but the amounts involved are small. At the same time, many channels of grant allocation lack transparency, and strong regions have a number of means for influencing the allocation of federal funds in their favor. For instance, the lion's share of federal funds appropriated for federal regional development programs ends up in the budgets of two republics, Bashkortostan and Tatarstan, which are already among the most developed Russian regions. Another example is Krasnoyarsk Krai, which received a special grant of US$76 million for its 2006 budget even though it is far from poor. Table 4.7 lists regions that received transfers for regional development.

Table 4.6 Federal Grants to Subnational Governments, 2005–07

Type of transfer	2005 Reported (US$ million)	2006 Budgeted (US$ million)	2006 Reported (US$ million)	2007 Budgeted (US$ million)
Equalization grants	6,597	7,606	8,681	10,212
Gap-filling subsidies	1,805	833	1,922	1,947
Cofinancing of social expenditure	879	994	994	1,391
Compensation for federal mandates	1,331	4,348	2,764	6,005
Capital transfers, of which	3,775	3,029	3,445	6,633
Regional development programs	*1,011*	*541*	*n.a.*	*2,914*
Other state programs	*2,140*	*1,323*	*n.a.*	*2,235*
Nonprogram	*604*	*1,165*	*n.a.*	*1,484*
Subnational finance reform grants	21	47	55	77
Operating transfers to special territories (irradiation sites, restricted access cities, research and development centers)	585	563	641	781
Ad hoc subsidies (Best-Run City Award, 2006–07 grants to Krasnoyarsk Oblast, to Koryak AO on earthquake consequences liquidation, 2005 transfer to the city of Sochi)	45	70	118	133
Other grants	1,804	855	3,582	3,565
Total	**16,911**	**17,351**	**22,201**	**30,745**
Intergovernmental transfers as a % of federal budget expenditures	*13.8%*	*12.2%*	*13.7%*	*14.3%*
Intergovernmental transfers as a % of GDP	*2.3%*	*2.1%*	*2.2%*	*2.6%*
Federal budget (US$ million)	*122,100*	*142,337*	*162,596*	*214,254*
GDP (US$ million)	*750,977*	*812,576*	*1,011,010*	*1,162,048*

Source: Authors' calculations based on Ministry of Finance federal budget reports; 2006–07 federal budget laws.

Table 4.7   Allocation of Transfers for Regional Development, 2005

Program or region	Amount (US$ million)
Republic of Tatarstan	446
Republic of Bashkortostan	216
Kaliningrad Oblast	36
Southern Russia	89
Far-eastern regions of Russia	33
Kuril Islands	8
Reducing disparities (formula-based allocation)	85
Chechen Republic	90
Other programs	8
Total	**1,011**

Source: Ministry of Finance data.

The grants that are allocated under the so-called national projects require special mention. Launched in December 2005, national projects are sets of targeted programs aimed at implementing the main constitutional guarantees that cover joint jurisdiction by the federal government and the regions—that is, education, health care, affordable housing, and agricultural development. When it comes to budget reporting, spending related to national projects is not reported under a separate heading. The projects are funded through capital transfers earmarked for construction or purchases of expensive equipment and subsidies for operating costs, such as special bonuses for teachers and general practitioners.

Despite the benefits of the programmatic approach that allows concentration of expenditures on priority needs and coordination of interdepartmental inputs, national projects are often at odds with the principles of decentralization, because some of the expenditure needs that are funded through national projects clearly fall under the jurisdiction of subnational governments. All regions receive both formula-based and other transfers. Subsidy recipients include Bashkortostan, Moscow, Tatarstan, and the domestic offshore zones, which suggests that political factors still influence the allocation of intergovernmental transfers.[16] In recent years, a negative transfer has been imposed on the regions by the federal center. According to a bilateral agreement signed between the federal government and the richest regions, such as the oil-extracting

---

16 For instance, the particularly high transfers to Koryak and Komi-Permyatsky Autonomous Okrugs had much to do with their mergers with the economically stronger neighbors.

Khanty-Mansi Autonomous Okrug (2006–07) and Moscow city (2007), these regions transfer money to the federal government. Appendix A shows the mix of revenues (own and transferred) available to regions after the allocation of all federal transfers.

Subnational Intergovernmental Relations

Intergovernmental relations, 1990–2005

Current relations between regional and local authorities in many respects closely resemble those that existed during the Soviet era and the early transition period of the 1990s, when these relationships acquired their distinctive region-specific features. The role of local governments started to change in 1990. Soviet law guaranteed the autonomy and independence of localities, and local council members (though not heads of administrations) were elected by popular vote. The law also determined council members' responsibilities and provided local councils with municipal property. Most importantly, the law assigned revenues to local governments that included shares of tax revenues from higher levels of government. The first Law on Local Self-Government (1991) went further and guaranteed elections not only for bodies of the representative branch of government, but also for heads of administrations. It also dissolved local executive committees, which had been the lowest link in the hierarchy of the regional administration. A list of taxes assigned to municipal budgets was drawn up in 1991, but the federal government retained the power to regulate the base and rate of these taxes and also retained the power to collect local taxes.

In 1995, the Law on General Principles of the Organization of Local Self-Government defined the status of local governments and their relations with regional authorities. The relations between regional and local governments were further altered by the 1997 Law on Financial Foundations of Local Self-Government, which established the average shares of federal taxes going to local governments. By this norm, the law limited the tax revenues of subjects of the federation (regions). In addition, it required a formula-based allocation of grants to localities, even though at that time hardly anyone grasped the legal interpretation of a formula, and as a result, the relevant provision of the law was simply ignored. During the 1990s, lawmakers' efforts were aimed primarily at limiting the influence of regional authorities on local governments. Then, in 2000, the Budget Code established local budgets as one of the three tiers of the intergovernmental fiscal system.

As noted earlier, before 2006, different organizational forms of local self-government had emerged in different regions (box 4.7), and these differences extended to some crucial areas, such as revenue sources, spending responsibilities, and even the way property was divided between regions and localities. Under the constitution and the Law on General Principles of the Organization of Local Self-Government, local self-governments were established in large cities, towns, rural raions, townships, and urban and rural settlements. In establishing such self-government, the authorities had to be mindful of historical and other local traditions. As of September 1, 2005, before the local government reform, Russia had about 29,130 local administrations, of which 13,652 were officially registered as municipal entities (Federal State Statistics Service 2005). Only 86.3 percent of the municipal entities had elected representative bodies of government; 85.4 percent

Box 4.7

Different Models of Local Self-Government

Before the local government reforms, in 50 regions local governments were established, mainly at the level of large cities and raions (the so-called "raion model" of local self-government; see Kurlyandskaya, Nikolayenko, and Golovanova 2001). In 13 regions, local self-governments were, for the most part, set up at the level of large cities and settlements (the "subraion model"), while 23 regions had a combination of raion and subraion types of local self-government (the "two-tier model").[17]

Typical examples of the raion model were Chuvash Republic, Novgorod Oblast, Primorski Krai, and Vologda Oblast. The republics of Bashkortostan and Tatarstan and Penza Oblast adopted the subraion model. The two-tier model was typical of Khabarovsk Krai; the Republic of Mordovia; and Astrakhan, Chelyabinsk, and Nizhny Novgorod Oblasts. These regions differed in terms of both their form of local self-government and the relationship between regional and local administrations.

These different forms of local self-government started to evolve in 1996–97, and the process was greatly influenced by the priorities of the incumbent

(continued)

---

17 A description of these three types of local governments is provided in an earlier section ("Assignment of Power and Local Government Reform, 2002–04").

Box 4.7 *(Continued)*

governors at that time. The heads and representative bodies of local government were elected on the basis of regional regulations that were passed in conformity with federal legislation. Governors attached a great deal of importance to building a government structure that could provide public services more efficiently and better control over spending and intergovernmental flows. They preferred the raion model of organization of local self-government, which allowed them to cut the number of local budgets at the regional level (depending on the region) and to simplify intergovernmental fiscal relations, including the calculation of transfers to local budgets.

For instance, because of the small number of local budgets in Novgorod Oblast, all local budgets could be prepared almost entirely by the regional finance committee (as opposed to local governments) and then be formally approved by the representative bodies of local self-government. Governor Mikhail Prussak's competent administrative style and more transparent methods of allocating financial resources among localities contributed toward this outcome, where decision making on local spending was largely in the hands of the oblast. In contrast, in neighboring Leningrad Oblast, the organization of local self-government at the raion level facilitated a greater degree of fiscal decentralization; the introduction of a transparent, formula-based mechanism for grant distribution; and the application of hard budget constraints on local spending.

In some cases, the development of local self-government was indeed an outcome of local initiative. In the overwhelming majority of cases, however, it was driven by what was desirable from the perspective of the governor of the region. A classic example is the development of local self-government in Tyumen Oblast. Under Governor Leonid Roketsky, local self-government had been established at the subraion level, except in the case of Zavodoukovski Raion, an oil-producing raion whose residents strongly resisted such a change. When Governor Sergei Sobyanin came to power, local self-government was introduced at the raion level through fair, legal procedures, but with one exception: Tyumenski Raion was divided into subraion municipalities.

Those governors who were fearful of opposition from elected heads of raions chose the subraion model and retained territorial subdivisions of the regional administration with appointed officials at the raion level. As a result, officials with strong management expertise remained under the governor's control at the raion level; becoming a key official in the more autonomous but less powerful rural settlements was never an attractive alternative.

had municipal charters, 74.6 percent possessed municipal property, and 81.6 percent had local budgets.

Russia's tax policy in the 1990s differed significantly from established norms of public finance, as demonstrated by how revenue sources were assigned across diverse local self-government entities. Because the tax legislation provided for a single list of local taxes, all local budgets had those taxes as sources of revenue. As a result, the same tax became a revenue base for large regional centers, municipal raions, and subraion municipalities alike. This system was problematic to maintain, especially for regions with local self-governments that were organized along the subraion principle. Local budgets in such regions either fully depended on one large taxpayer or had no tax base whatsoever. Fragmentation of the territorial structure of local governments caused considerable disparity among local budgets in terms of tax bases, leading some localities to have excessive revenue bases while others to depend largely on transfers from the region. However, if subraion municipalities were merged into a municipal raion, the disparities within the raion were likely to disappear without intervention by the region.

Most of the tax-sharing rates for regional budgets were established for one fiscal year. Every region retained the same centrally established share of tax collections for its budget, which it could use at its own discretion. A portion of collections was retained in regional budgets, and some was transferred to localities at the regional administration's discretion. Generally, more than 30 percent of federal taxes accruing to regions were transferred to local budgets. In addition to federal taxes, regions could transfer any regional taxes to localities, and the federal government did not set rates at which federal taxes had to be shared with localities, except that 50 percent of regional enterprise property taxes had to be transferred to all local budgets.[18]

Unlike the federal government, regional governments were free to assign different shares and rates of regulating taxes to different municipalities. Only a few regions had started to apply uniform sharing rates to all localities. Moreover, tax-sharing rates that changed from year to year turned localities' tax revenues into tax transfers—that is, to grants transferred in the form of tax revenues. The distribution of regulating taxes among localities was not linked to localities' actual needs and preceded the allocation of grants. The shares of regulating taxes to be assigned to a

---

18 Some regions, such as Rostov Oblast, broke this mandate, leaving the city of Rostov-on-Don, for example, with 36 to 40 percent of collections in 1997–2000.

locality in a particular fiscal year were negotiated between local and regional officials, with each party striving to grab a bigger share of the taxes. Rich municipalities with a well-developed tax base were the most active in scrambling for their share of regulating taxes, while poor municipalities were assigned 100 percent of shared taxes each year. Even under this sharing arrangement, the tax revenues of poor municipalities were so small that transfers from the regional budget remained their main source of revenues (Kurlyandskaya and Golovanova 2006; Martinez-Vazquez, Timofeev, and Boex 2006).

In the 1990s, the distribution of equalization transfers among local budgets was designed to achieve a balance between revenue sources and spending responsibilities in every region. In virtually every region, grants were calculated as the difference between the so-called normative budget of a municipality and its expected revenues. In some regions, regional governments developed and legislatively fixed spending norms for municipalities. In some cases, those norms were used exclusively for calculating grants, while in others they were used as the compulsory minimum local spending levels. However, the final amount of grants was usually established through negotiations. These negotiations often took the form of regions complaining about municipalities' weak tax collection efforts and high expenditure, and municipalities complaining that their expenditure responsibilities far exceeded their revenues.

In 2000, the federal Ministry of Finance approved recommendations regulating intergovernmental fiscal relations. The recommendations included methodologies for formalizing the calculation of grants in a way that would not create perverse incentives for localities to under-report their revenues and over-report their expenditures. However, the regions took their time applying transparent methods to intergovernmental fiscal relations, because those methods would inevitably have diminished the role of regional financial authorities in managing the grants approval process. The strong push to apply formula-based methods came from the federal government, which started to use such methods as of 2000 to calculate grants for the regions. In addition, during the World Bank project on Reforming Regional Finances, the formalization of fiscal relations was a criterion for participation in the project.

As a result, by 2003, about one-third of all the regions had started to use a formula-based approach, including the Republic of Chuvashia; Krasnoyarsk Krai; and Astrakhan, Chelyabinsk, Leningrad, Rostov, and Vladimir Oblasts. Moreover, a few regions legislated the use of this methodology. Applying the methodology proved to be more difficult in regions where local self-governments were organized along the subraion or two-tier principle because of the difficulty of obtaining critical information from every agent of the chain. By 2005, the Budget Code included a requirement for formula-based transfer allocations and sharing rates for federal taxes, while the lists of local government issues were already established in the 2003 Law on General Principles of the Organization of Local Self-Government. As a result of these reforms, the system of intergovernmental relations became more stable and transparent but less flexible, in that the regions lost their power to design their own systems of local self-government that best suited the existing local needs and conditions.

Intergovernmental relations as of 2006

As table 4.5 shows, local budgets depend heavily on grants from higher-level governments. The Budget Code regulates the allocation of transfers from regional and local budgets: it establishes the main kinds of transfers, the terms of their allocation, the principles underlying the provision of equalization transfers and compensation for delegated responsibilities, and the principles for budget credit arrangements.

Transfers from regional budgets include much the same kinds of transfers as from the federal government to regional governments (equalization grants, gap-filling subsidies, compensation for regional and federal mandates, and the like). The Budget Code sets the rates for taxes shared between the federal and local governments, but the regions may pass their own laws for establishing additional sharing rates with local governments.[19]

Before 2005, the federal government viewed the formula-based methodology for allocating equalization grants as desirable but did not mandate its use. However, its use has been mandated since 2005. What is more, the Budget Code envisages the allocation of equalization transfers on the basis of tax capacity indicators and differences in the composition of the population by age group and socioeconomic, climatic, geographic, and other factors that affect per capita public service costs. The Law on General Principles of the Organization of Local Self-Government permitted the regions to postpone the introduction of a transparent formula for transfer allocation to local governments until 2009 so that the regions could decide whether to introduce the new intergovernmental arrangements in 2006 or to introduce them gradually during 2006–08.

---

19 According to the Budget Code, these sharing rates should be unified for all raions or
   for all settlements in the region.

The Budget Code also provides for the collection of negative transfers from local governments to regional budgets; thus, if a municipality's estimated per capita tax revenues are more than double the average local tax capacity, the region may take up to 50 percent of the excess for reallocation among poorer municipalities.[20]

Regions continue to resort to different ways of equalizing per capita budget revenues across municipalities because of the lack of a strong methodological basis and for political reasons. For some regions, granting equal access to government services for all people within the region, whatever municipality they live in, is the key objective. For others, the primary aim of the equalization strategy is to provide local governments with incentives to develop their own revenue base. Municipal raions also have the right to equalize the budgets of settlements.

Disparities across localities are sometimes no less striking than those across regions. Typically, an extremely rich municipality is one that has a large enterprise generating big profits. A significant number of these enterprises are oil- or gas-producing companies, manufacturers, electricity-generating facilities, or producers of alcoholic beverages. In oil-producing regions, the richest municipalities are those where crude oil is extracted. Table 4.8 shows the sources of subnational government revenues in three typical regions—Amur Oblast, Astrakhan Oblast, and Stavropol Krai—that are neither particularly wealthy nor particularly poor. In terms of per capita own revenues, in 2006, Amur Oblast ranked 50th of all regions. Stavropol Krai and Astrakhan Oblast ranked 28th and 61st, respectively. Figures 4.7 to 4.10 show per capita budget revenue spread across municipalities in selected regions.[21]

In Astrakhan Oblast (figure 4.7), own revenues are evenly distributed with the exception of Krasnoyarski Raion (shown on the far right of the x axis), where a gas-producing company is located.

Relatively low disparities in the distribution of own revenues in Amur Oblast (figure 4.8) are reduced even more following the receipt of equalization transfers from the oblast budget.

Stavropol Krai (figure 4.9) is one of the few Russian regions that had a two-tier system of municipalities even before the enactment of the new law on local self-government. As a result, consolidated budget data are available

20 Nine regions used this authority in 2007.
21 Figures 4.7 to 4.10 resemble figure 4.6 for federal equalization grants, but instead of the ratio of the fiscal capacity index to the expenditure needs index, per capita fiscal capacity in U.S. dollars is presented on the vertical axis.

Table 4.8   Sources of Subnational Governments' Revenues in Amur and Astrakhan Oblasts and Stavropol Krai, 2006

	Revenue (US$ per capita)		
Item	Astrakhan Oblast	Stavropol Krai	Amur Oblast
Local revenues before transfers	155	116	152
Local revenues after transfers from regional government	324	308	576
Revenues of subnational governments (regional + local) before transfers from the federal government	461	350	573
Total subnational revenues after federal transfers	595	499	890

Source: Authors' calculations based on the Ministry of Finance regional and local budget 12-month execution reports as of January 1, 2007.

Figure 4.7   Astrakhan Oblast, Raions and Cities, 2006

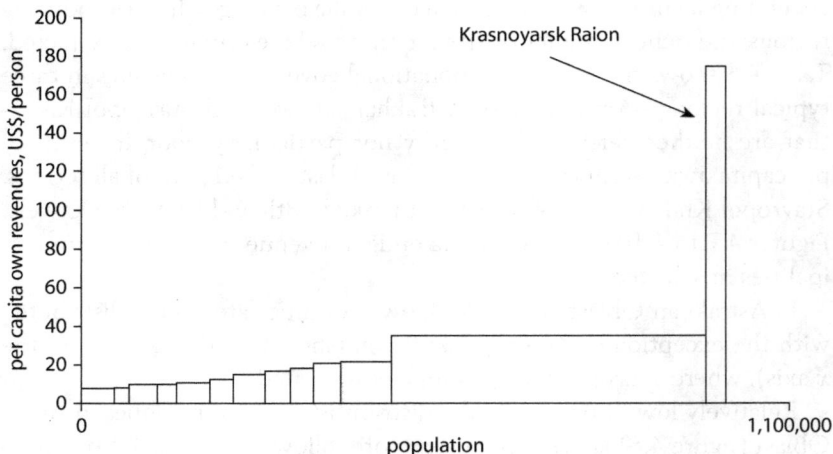

Source: Authors' calculations based on regional and local budget execution reports.

not only at the level of cities and raions (including settlements) for Stavropol Krai, but also for individual settlements within raions (figure 4.10).

Figure 4.10 shows the per capita budget revenue spread (from own taxes, before transfers) across settlements in Stavropol Krai. Stavropol city is a recipient of both settlement revenues and revenues assigned to subregional cities and raions. As a settlement, it receives about US$40 per

Figure 4.8   Amur Oblast, Raions and Cities, 2006

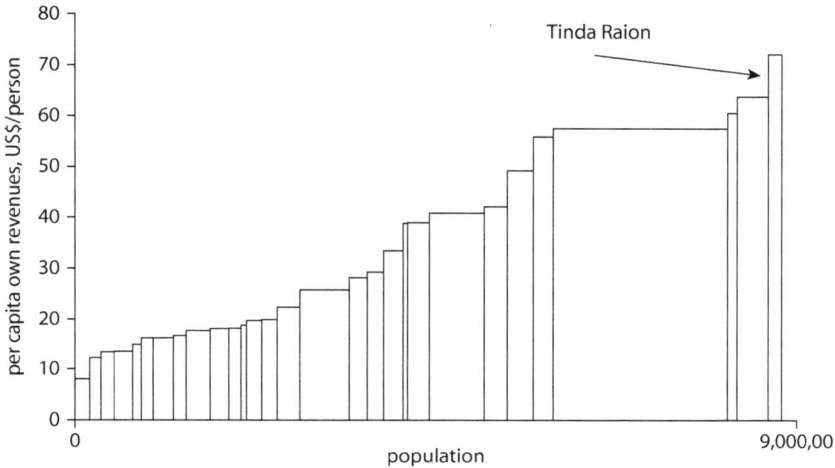

Source: Authors' calculations based on regional and local budget execution reports.

Figure 4.9   Stavropol Krai, Raions and Cities, 2006

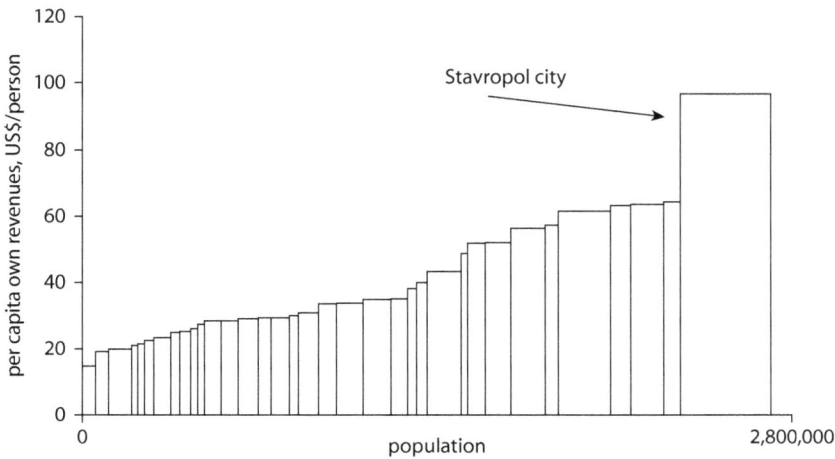

Source: Authors' calculations based on regional and local budget execution reports.

capita from its own-revenue sources, and as a city it gets an additional US$100 per capita from own-revenue sources. The average annual revenues in Stavropol Krai in 2006 after the receipt of federal transfers amounted to US$499 per person (see table 4.8).

Figure 4.10   Stavropol Krai, Settlements and Cities, 2006

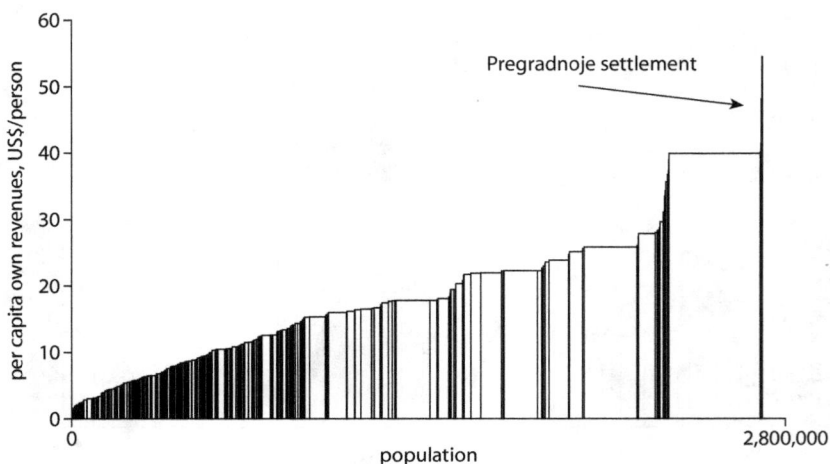

Source: Authors' calculations based on regional and local budget execution reports.

Subnational Borrowing

The Budget Code places some restrictions on borrowing by subnational governments: a region's deficit cannot exceed 15 percent of its revenues, and a local government's deficit cannot exceed 10 percent of its revenues, excluding transfers from higher levels of government and the proceeds from sales of property.[22] These limits on borrowing and debt amounts were included in the federal legislation following the 1998 financial crisis, when a number of regions found themselves close to bankruptcy. Regions rarely disregard these requirements.

At present, the market for regional bonds remains relatively small, but it has been exhibiting high growth rates in recent years (figure 4.11). In 2004, 49 of the 89 regions raised funds by issuing regional bonds or redeeming ones that had been issued earlier. Moscow city bonds account for a significant portion of the market. As of May 31, 2007, the total amount of regional and municipal bonds placed in the market was US$8.0 billion, of which more than half—about US$4.2 billion—were Moscow city bonds.

Based on the Budget Code's ceiling for borrowing, the potential size of the market of subnational obligations equals US$142 billion, an amount

---

22 Amendments to the Budget Code set stricter rules for subnational governments with a high share of federal financial assistance in their total budget revenues (see tables 3.2 and 3.3).

Figure 4.11   Subnational Government Bonds Market, 2002–07

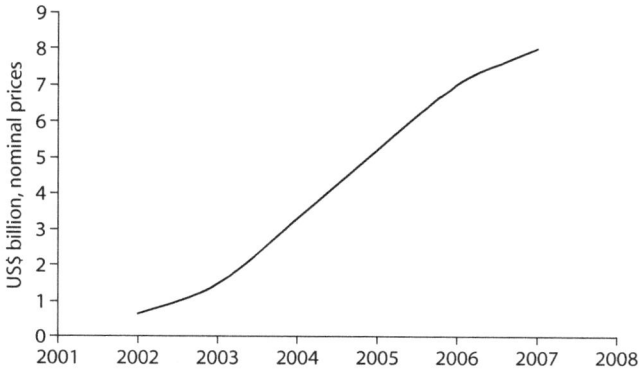

Source: http://www.cbonds.info.

roughly equivalent to total own revenues of subnational governments in fiscal year 2006. However, a more realistic estimate of the potential size of the subnational bond market is 40 to 60 percent of that figure.

An amendment to the Budget Code in year 2000 forbids regional and local governments from taking loans in a foreign currency, except when new loans in foreign currency are intended to refinance already existing loans.[23] As of June 2007, only the city of Moscow had outstanding bonds in foreign currency (Eurobonds), but a few other cities, including St. Petersburg and Krasnoyarsk, had outstanding foreign currency bank loans.

An alternative way for regions to obtain access to foreign currency loans is the reassignment of loans by the federal Ministry of Finance. The ministry obtains loans in foreign currency under its own guarantees and reassigns them to regions in rubles. At the end of 2006, the total outstanding amount of such loans owed by the regions to the Ministry of Finance was about US$190 million.

As of May 31, 2007, of more than 24,000 local governments, only 21 had issued bonds. The practice of issuing bonds is more widespread among regions and 40 of them had issued bonds. The share of local governments in the subnational bond market is only 3.3 percent. According

---

23 The Budget Code also imposes several other important restrictions on regional governments, including the requirement to register the issuance of regional bonds at the Federal Ministry of Finance, the limitation on borrowing only for investment purposes, and the assignment of a government agency with the sole authorization to carry out these borrowings.

to recent estimates, only 80 cities are financially strong enough to be able to issue bonds, and 23 of them have already done so.

Another type of debt instrument that subnational governments use is bank credits. Two types of banks offer loans to regional and municipal governments: (a) leading domestic banks that have an extended network of local offices (these banks intend to significantly increase their lending to subnational governments in the near future), and (b) regional banks with a large share of regional government ownership. In the balance sheets of these regional banks, the share (as a percentage of the total) of loans given to regional and municipal administrations exceeds the share given to corporations by a factor of 1.5. Usually, the loans extended by such banks bear a nonmarket interest rate that is either abnormally low or abnormally high.

The federal Ministry of Finance carefully monitors regional governments' debt and deficits and is planning to pass an insolvency law that would require the implementation of emergency financial management controls in case such governments exceed their debt limits. As noted earlier, such occurrences are rare. In 2005, the most widespread breach of financial discipline identified by the Ministry of Finance was overdue liabilities on the part of regions: 50 of 89 subjects of the federation had outstanding liabilities, but to date none has been sanctioned for this default.

As a result of the restrictions, regional governments' debt burden has continued to shrink since the end of the 1990s, and as of the end of 2008, it was equivalent to less than 2 percent of the GDP. The consolidated regional debt is 15 percent of total regional government spending. Spending by Moscow city accounts for roughly 20 percent of total regional government spending, and the city is responsible for the bulk of regional government debt.

Official figures on regional governments' debt and budget deficits are estimated on a cash basis and do not take accrued liabilities into account. In some regions in the 1990s, public employee wage arrears carried over from previous years, overdue debts of public enterprises (accounts payable), or both, although not shown in budget execution reports, still constituted a sizable share of regional governments' liabilities. In the mid to late 1990s, subnational wage arrears increased to an equivalent of 2 percent of the GDP, although in recent years, such arrears shrank to about 0.01 percent of the GDP, largely because of the favorable economic climate caused mainly by massive petroleum revenues accrued to the national budget.

In April 2007, President Putin signed a number of amendments to the Budget Code pertaining to regional governments' finances. One amendment grants subjects of the federation the right to take foreign loans as of January 1, 2011, although the borrowing procedures have yet to be determined. Granting the regions permission to borrow in foreign currency will increase foreign currency risks and may interfere with the central bank's currency exchange policy. Compared with the extent of hard currency borrowing by the corporate sector, however, the extent of future borrowing by subnational governments will be small and the demand for borrowing in hard currency could be more modest than expected on the part of most regional governments. The cost of borrowing in rubles, even if it remains higher than the cost of borrowing in hard currency, may still be attractive because the professional skills required for foreign currency risk management are still absent in most regions.

In June 2007, the federal government set up the Development Bank to finance public investment. Regional and local governments may be able to borrow from this bank to finance their development projects, although the bank may focus mostly on large-scale, national projects and thus avoid dealing with small municipal borrowers for which the transaction costs could be significantly higher.

Another way to boost local borrowing that has been proposed but is still under discussion is to set up local government borrowing pools that would issue bonds in their own name and extend credits to their members. Before implementing an arrangement of this kind, the fiduciary responsibilities of local governments and the role of the federal government (that is, in relation to oversight and responsibilities) would have to be carefully reviewed. Some authors have pointed to the importance of a reliable system of intergovernmental revenue coupled with a strong own-revenue system as important preconditions for subnational borrowing (Alam, Titov, and Petersen 2004). At the same time, incentives for local policy makers to borrow at will need to be limited, because their desire to borrow is often driven by narrow, short-term political goals. Another critical requirement would be for subnational governments to have modern budgetary systems and the capacity to design, implement, and monitor budgets, all of which are important for formulating reliable revenue and expenditure projections prior to making such borrowing decisions (Tanzi 1995).[24]

---

24 International experience on managing subnational borrowing indicates that a combination of a rule-based approach (such as the golden rule on allowing subnational borrowing mainly for investment projects) and a market-based approach (which includes independent external auditing, debt rating agencies, and so forth to further enhance transparency and accountability) will work best.

CHAPTER 5

Federalism Russian Style

In 2005, the federal government finished implementing its Fiscal Federalism Program, which it had started in 2002. The program was among the few that the government had more or less successfully completed. The resulting assignment of responsibilities, however, lacks the full clarity that is required, and the existing regional government structure also remains a far cry from the concept of federalism in general and of fiscal federalism in particular.

In the course of implementing the program, the federal government promulgated several important laws (see table 3.1) to clarify the expenditure assignment between federal and regional authorities (amendments to Federal Law No. 184-FZ, July 2003); to develop local self-government (Federal Law No.131-FZ, October 2003); and to bring the rest of federal legislation in line with the new assignment of responsibilities across the federal government and subnational governments (Federal Law No. 122-FZ, August 2004). These laws resulted in the centralization of resources (see figure 3.2), but political power remained decentralized, and the regions retained discretion over several important functions,

---

Some parts of this chapter were published in Kurlyandskaya and Deryugin (2007).

such as health care and education, where the federal government promised not to interfere.[1]

In September 2004, the federal government embarked on a serious reform effort aimed at concentrating its political power, and President Putin started to appoint governors (see box 1.1). The new procedure for appointing governors is subject to approval by the regional legislative assemblies and was to replace gubernatorial elections. As a result, a return to further decentralization of responsibilities has become possible, but with a new twist—strangely the responsibilities are to be now "decentralized" through deconcentration, given that governors have now become an integral part of the federal government's executive power. Federal inspectors under the plenipotentiary representatives of the president in each okrug and the Main Control Department of the Administrative Board of the President exercise control over governors. This proposed new model does not promote greater accountability by subnational executive bodies to the populations they are expected to serve.

The current strategy of decentralization can therefore be summarized as follows: the federal government appoints regional authorities, assigns them responsibilities along with corresponding resources, and keeps their spending under strict control. If public funds are misappropriated and the situation in a region deteriorates, the president has the tools to reverse the situation. The danger inherent in this strategy is that once the federal government starts to exercise control over the execution of federal responsibilities by the regions, it may be tempted to take under its control those functions that fall under joint jurisdiction by the federal government and the regions that had previously been assigned to the regions. The danger is quite real because the number of additional functions assigned to the regions is far greater than those assigned to the regions previously and with which the federal government promised not to interfere.

As mentioned previously, one of the specific features of Russian federalism is that subnational governments have little revenue autonomy. On average, the share of revenues in the consolidated budget of a region over which the region had some level of control did not exceed 40 percent of its total revenues between 1999 and 2004 and 50 percent in 2005–06. In seven regions, this share is no more than 10 percent. The share of revenues from regional and local taxes in consolidated subnational budgets dropped to 11 percent in 2005. With no tax authority of their own— and thus no instruments of control over tax collection—subnational

---

1 Federal government was *not* as good as its word: it interfered in subnational issues through amendments to the legislation and grants for high-priority national projects.

governments currently do not have control even over the three regional taxes and two local ones that are assigned to them.

Moreover, federal taxes that are due to subnational budgets cannot be regarded as "own" revenues because regional authorities cannot regulate the collections of these taxes any more than they can regulate the size of federal transfers that are due for subnational governments. The bargaining over the assignment of expenditure responsibilities between the regions and the federal government is essentially bargaining over money, because the more expenditure responsibilities that are assigned to the regions, the more funds they will receive from the federal government in the form of shared taxes and transfers.

Because regional and local budgets are composed of federal taxes and federal transfers rather than regional and local taxes collected from citizens to whom regional and local governments deliver public services, people do not hold subnational governments accountable. Moreover, the main taxpayers are businesses, not individuals, and therefore, governors are more interested in attracting businesses into their jurisdictions than in improving the services consumed largely by residents.

After the Budget Code had permanently assigned own and federal tax sources to the subnational level, subnational authorities became less dependent on annual budgetary decisions by the federal government. Before the Budget Code assigned shared taxes on a permanent basis, the shares could be changed each year by the federal Budget Law. Even after Budget Code's "permanent" assignment of tax sources to subnational governments, they could still be changed by the sole initiative of the federal government, as a result of several amendments to the Budget Code introduced during the past two years. Therefore, these amendments have not strengthened the revenue autonomy of the regions to any noticeable degree. Regional revenues still do not depend on the tax effort of a region, and its taxes still constitute an insignificantly small share of the region's total revenues.

The same is true of the equalization transfer formula. The use of a formula-based approach, as opposed to negotiated arrangements, to transfer allocation would seem to provide the regions financial independence from the center. This is not exactly true, because the federal government devises the formula and introduces annual amendments to the formula. Consequently, regions' revenues had not become significantly more predictable even after the introduction of a formula-based transfer mechanism. The recent studies have failed to establish a statistically meaningful relation between changes in a region's spending needs and changes in the size of the grants allocated to it. Revenues of the subjects of the Russian Federation could have become more predictable after the transition to a three-year budget in 2008 when resulting equalization transfer allocation's were fixed for three years. However, the financial crisis has changed the rules of the game and the system of intergovernmental fiscal relations—which were developed during a period of sustained economic growth—could undergo significant change in a falling economy.[2]

The Impact of the Crisis

Although Russia has accumulated a vast war chest of foreign currency reserves during the recent period of high oil and other natural resource prices, which could potentially last for few more years, its excessive dependence on these exports makes Russia's economy much more vulnerable to a worldwide recession than those of some of the other emerging markets with large reserves, such as China and India. A majority of Russia's Fortune 100 companies in terms of their market capitalization operate in oil, gas, and other natural resource sectors. In 2007, for example, 78.5 percent of Russia's exports were oil, fuel (coal) and gas (Powell 2008). Only a handful of them are in other important sectors such as manufacturing or high-tech.[3]

A declining resource base will likely have serious implications for intergovernmental relations. Already there are indications that subnational revenues are dropping considerably, compared to a year ago—by 17 percent on average during the period between October 2008 and February 2009.

---

2 Amendments to the Budget Code that were introduced by Federal Law No. 58-FZ on April 9, 2009, stipulate that the part of the federal budget related to the planning period (that is, the two budget years beyond the next budget year) can be canceled. Following these amendments, part of the current federal budget concerning the years 2010 and 2011 was indeed canceled by the Federal Law No. 76-FZ, which was introduced on April 28, 2009. However, according to the finance minister, the planning for 2010 to 2012 will be carried out within the three-year expenditure framework and will be done from scratch (that is, without using the part of the budget that was canceled). The budget for 2010 to 2012 will be presented to the Duma in October 2009. Formally, it should be presented no later than August 26, but the date is expected to be changed to October 1; this change is not yet reflected in the Budget Code, but the process has already started. The regions will conduct the medium-term budget planning by themselves, and they will choose between a one-year or three-year budget on their own. Most of the regions have already adopted medium-term expenditure frameworks, but it is possible that they will amend the relevant regional legislation and return to one-year budgeting.

3 Even in the absence of the current global economic crisis, the Russian economy remained vulnerable to the Dutch Disease in which resource movement and spending effects cause a decline in the nonbooming tradable sector and an appreciation of the real exchange rate.

In contrast, the federal revenue declined by 13 percent during the same period. On a yearly basis, subnational revenues are likely to decline even further. The country's economy has shrunk 9.5 percent in the first quarter of 2009, while the 2009 budget is based on a contraction of 2.2 percent. Subnational debt repayment liability has been increasing (by 25 percent in 2009 and by another 35 percent in 2010) because of high levels of short-term debt in the current portfolio, half of which will require refinancing. In contrast to the precrisis period, the yield on regional bonds is higher than the yield on corporate bonds, indicating a growing uncertainty among investors of the recovery of the corporate sector.

Although the limit for the accumulated debt for regions is set at 100 percent of current own revenue (excluding intergovernmental transfers), the debt of half of Russia's regions, as reported on January 1, 2009, has been 15 percent of their own revenues. Hence, more than half of the regions still have very little debt. Only 7 out of 83 regions have a debt level that is higher than 45 percent of their revenue.[4] During the period between 1996 and 2008, while the federal government's debt as a percentage of GDP fluctuated between 152 percent in 1998 and 8 percent in 2008, the regional government debt remained around 2 to 4 percent, except in 2000, when it increased to 6 percent (see figure 5.1).

According to the preliminary estimates of the Ministry of Finance, the consolidated budgets of the Russian Federation subjects (regions) will, in 2009, lose roughly Rub 600 billion to Rub 700 billion (18 percent from the previous year). Personal income tax revenues accrued to regional budgets are expected to decrease, but to a lesser extent than the decline in corporate profit tax, simply because during a crisis corporate profits tend to fall more steeply than do personal incomes; as a result, revenues from the profit tax—which constitute about 30 percent of subnational budgets—will likely decline sharply. Hence, the regional budget deficit in 2009 is projected to grow about 15 times from the previous year to reach Rub 800 billion.

Regions with developed economies, where the largest taxpayers are businesses—steel, coal, large machine-building plants, and so forth—will be the first to suffer. The most affected Russian Federation subjects will include Belgorod, Chelyabinsk, Lipetsk, Omsk Orenburg, and Vologda Oblasts and Krasnoyarsk Krai. They are largely donor regions whose revenues have sharply increased recently, and the newly developed vast

---

4 These 15 percent and 45 percent thresholds were chosen by the Ministry of Regional Development, from which these figures were taken.

Figure 5.1   Accumulated Debt of Federal and Regional (Subnational) Governments
(as a percentage of GDP)

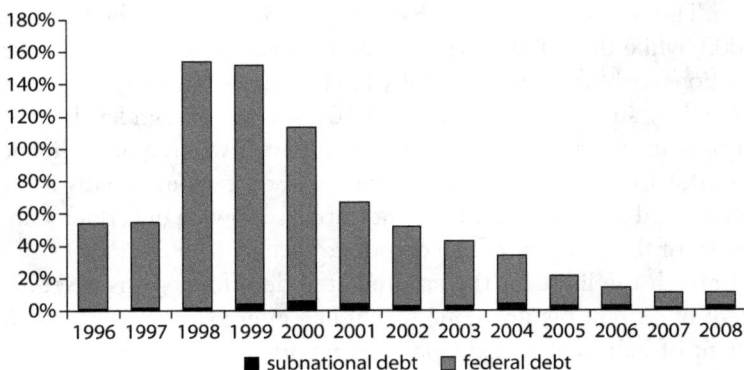

Source: Authors' calculations based on Ministry of Finance data.

infrastructure networks will incur heavy maintenance costs. The changes in oil prices will continue to affect Russia's oil-producing regions, including two of the richest regions: Tyumen Oblast and Khanty-Mansi Autonomous Okrug. In January 2009, the tax and nontax revenues in these regions were roughly 70 percent of those from a year ago, while the regional average for the same period was 83 percent.

From January to March 2009, regional arrears grew up by 50 percent, and with the anticipated rise in inflation, the cost of borrowing for the regions will significantly go up. The rating agencies have been reducing the credit ratings of the regions because of the potential liquidity risks the regions will likely to face if the current crisis further deepens. The federal government is expected to lower the threshold of regional outstanding debt from 30 percent to 10 percent as part of its crisis management strategy. Furthermore, concerted efforts by the federal Ministry of Finance to improve public finance management in subnational governments may likely to institute better debt management systems in the Russian regions. If the federal government fails to manage the crisis well, the chances are that once the reserves are depleted, Russia could again plunge into an era marked by arrears and a barter economy, defaults by regional governments, and poor quality of public services all around.

Since then, the federal center has accumulated substantial reserves (for example, in extrabudgetary funds such as the stabilization fund) during the period of high oil prices; thus, it is capable of supporting the regions, at least in the short run. The current federal Budget Law (adopted at the end of 2008) provides for Rub 1,335 billion to cover intergovernmental transfers. The amendments to the budget add another Rub 300 billion to achieve the same objective, out of which Rub 150 billion will be provided to balance the budgets (instead of Rub 43 billion, as planned earlier), and the other Rub 150 billion will be used to provide budget loans (instead of Rub 20 billion, as planned earlier), with the period of budget loans to be extended from one to three years. The regions will also receive additional targeted subventions to support anti-crisis measures, which include those for reducing unemployment and its negative consequences. Because most of the regional investment projects are cofinanced by grants from the federal budget, a decision was made to allow a proportional reduction of the matching funds from the regions to cofinance those expenditures.

However, if petroleum prices continue to hover around US$50 to US$55 for the next year or two, Russia will find it difficult to continue to support subnational governments at the same level as prescribed by the 2008 Budget Law. The 2010–12 budget will be based on the conservative estimates that the price of oil barrel will be US$50 in 2010, US$52 in 2011, and US$53 in 2012. The federal revenue during this period will likely to be significantly lower than it was in the previous year, and already some disturbing trends are appearing on the horizon. As the Federal Tax Service reported on May 25, 2009, fiscal revenue from taxes and other dues fell by about a fifth between January and April of this year, and the budget deficit is expected to reach at least 7 percent of GDP in 2009 (Kelly 2009).

An Uncertain Future for Intergovernmental Reforms?

Not all intergovernmental fiscal reforms implemented over the past two decades have gone astray or are likely to be reversed in the foreseeable future. The sustainability of some of these reforms so far may provide hope that they will strengthen the institutional framework for further intergovernmental reforms in the future. The elimination of unfunded mandates and a better clarification of tax assignment, including long-term and symmetric assignment of shared taxes on a derivation basis, were key achievements. Similarly, the adoption of an equalization formula based on per capita revenues adjusted for the cost of public services in different regions was critical for providing some stability and transparency to the process. The federal government's assistance to subnational governments to improve their public financial and debt management systems is another reform measure that is starting to show some positive results in the regions. However, the current crisis hangs over intergovernmental relations as a sword of Damocles indicating the possibility of a further tightening of federal government's grip on subnational units. What remains uncertain is whether it will provide further impetus to already visible attempts to reverse some of the decentralization reforms, especially in terms of devolving political and administrative powers to subnational governments.

When discussing federalism issues in Russia, it is difficult to avoid the issue of corruption. Various organizations that have estimated the level of corruption agree that it is fairly high (Information Science for Democracy Foundation 2005; Yakovlev and Zhuravskaya 2006). There are many reasons for this outcome, including Russia's communist history and traditions, the low salaries of government officials, and the visible impunity of those who repeatedly engage in corrupt business and administrative practices. However, none of these are valid reasons for the growing extent of corruption, which could have far-reaching implications on fiscal decentralization reforms and the country's overall economic growth.

In the area of public finance, the high level of corruption in the regions is rooted in part in the federal government's intergovernmental transfer policy, which lacks transparent and formalized procedures for allocating huge amounts of money. This failure motivates regions to establish both formal and informal contractual relations with the federal government. Furthermore, to avoid reducing the amount of federal transfers, regions have a tendency to hide some of their revenue sources. To date, no one has been punished for engaging in such activities. Corruption is also rooted in the existing institutional structure, whereby regions and localities have no legal means of adjusting their per capita tax revenues.

Corruption may become even worse as a result of the enactment of the 2003 law on local self-government, which does not allow municipalities to own property that is not directly related to the performance of their functions. Municipalities have already started to strip themselves of such property, selling it to hastily created firms that—although formally not owned by the local governments—are in reality controlled by them. A significant portion of a municipal government's economy is probably linked to such "shadow" arrangements for sources of revenue.

The pertinent questions are whether fiscal federalism is possible in the absence of political decentralization and whether political decentralization is possible without some degree of revenue autonomy. Opinions among those who have closely observed Russia's transition vary (Kurlyandskaya and Deryugin 2007). Some argue that Russia's recent move toward a unitary state is only temporary, and its fiscal federalism reforms—including the greater financial autonomy of the regions because of the (albeit scarce) revenue sources assigned to them, the formula-driven allocation of equalization transfers, and the various federal funds that have been set up to allocate targeted transfers to the regions—will pave the way for enhanced political federalism. Others argue that genuine reforms in the areas of fiscal federalism and local self-governance are impossible without subnational units having revenue autonomy and that a genuine move toward fiscal federalism cannot coexist with the increasing tendency to strengthen the vertical axis of executive power.[5]

The most likely outcome, given current trends, is a return to the asymmetrical model of federalism, although with a new face.[6] In the 1990s, strong regions (for example, regions with vast endowments of natural resources) received additional powers under bilateral agreements with the federal government. In contrast, the model that is used today involves limiting the discretion of the poorest regions in using their financial resources (see table 3.2). More specifically, one of the main issues being debated by Russian policy makers today concerns changing the fiscal equalization policy. Many politicians believe that the poorest regions, which depend on federal grants for more than half their revenues, should come under emergency financial control of the federal government and that the bulk of federal support extended to such regions should be spent on capital projects with positive externalities that cut across regional borders. However, these kinds of regional policies are more appropriate for a centralized state than for a federative state.

Is it an accurate conclusion, therefore, that efforts to develop intergovernmental fiscal relations have been in vain since fiscal federalism will inevitably wither away because of the lack of political federalism? Or could steps be taken to guarantee the financial autonomy of subjects of

---

5 Bardhan and Mookherjee (2006) identify three types of decentralization. Type A is the big-bang approach, with a simultaneous economic and political decentralization, as has occurred in Bolivia, Indonesia, and post-1994 South Africa. In type B, decentralization leads to a comprehensive political devolution, while economic devolution remains uneven, as has occurred in Brazil and India. The design of decentralization reforms in the Russian Federation has more in common with type C—where administrative and economic devolution are more pronounced than political devolution—than with the other two types. China, Pakistan, Uganda, and pre-1994 South Africa are some examples of the type C design of decentralization. Still, the Russian experience is far from a perfect fit of this type because it has the unique feature of locally elected officials who have been subordinate to upper-level government officials. In contrast, in Pakistan, state bureaucrats are subordinate to elected local officials (at least *de jure*), while in China it is exactly the opposite.

6 An asymetric model of federalism contradicts the constitutional guarantee of equal treatment of all subjects of the federation.

the federation that will still work to reinforce intergovernmental fiscal reforms? Whether Russia is able to preserve some of the positive, albeit few, developments of a nearly two-decade-long decentralization reform effort depends largely on the willingness of the current political regime. The other alternative is to hope for a strong push from the bottom—from subnational governments—for a continuation of reforms to grant them more autonomy. This latter alternative appears highly unlikely given the increasingly authoritative manner in which the federal government influences intergovernmental fiscal reforms. Although, as Dostoyevsky reminds us, a just cause should not be ruined by a few mistakes, an appropriate question to be posed in this context is whether the "few" mistakes are large enough to cause an irreparable damage to reforms that are already in place and that were introduced through many trials and errors over the past two decades. This is an outcome that Russia may want to avoid at all costs.

Appendix A

Russian Federation's Constituent States: Basic Facts

Map location	Constituent states	Area (1,000 sq. km.)	GDP (US$/per capita, 2005)	Population, (1000, 2006)	Title ethnicity[a] (% of total population, 2002)	Russians (% of total population, 2002)	Own subnational budget revenues (US$ per capita, 2006)	Own and assigned subnational budget revenues (US$ per capita, 2006)	Transfers from federal budget per capita (US$, 2006)	Total subnational budget revenues per capita[b] (US$, 2006)
	Central Federal Okrug									
1	Belgorod Oblast	27.1	3,383	1,512	—	92.9	379	623	117	741
2	Bryansk Oblast	34.9	1,744	1,346	—	96.3	137	304	193	497
3	Vladimir Oblast	29.0	2,072	1,487	—	94.7	200	426	124	549
4	Voronezh Oblast	52.4	2,045	2,334	—	94.1	184	378	118	495
5	Ivanovo Oblast	23.9	1,452	1,115	—	93.7	194	382	218	599
6	Kaluga Oblast	29.9	2,552	1,022	—	93.5	216	510	137	648
7	Kostroma Oblast	60.1	2,210	717	—	95.6	158	394	148	542
8	Kursk Oblast	29.8	2,559	1,199	—	95.9	221	410	119	529
9	Lipetsk Oblast	24.1	4,294	1,190	—	95.8	601	841	51	892
10	Moscow Oblast	46.0	3,692	6,630	—	91.0	505	903	101	1,003
11	Oryol Oblast	24.7	2,416	842	—	95.3	167	368	137	504
12	Ryazan Oblast	39.6	2,494	1,195	—	94.6	217	461	102	563
13	Smolensk Oblast	49.8	2,362	1,019	—	93.4	188	417	90	508
14	Tambov Oblast	34.3	1,984	1,145	—	96.5	153	314	190	504
15	Tver Oblast	84.1	2,343	1,425	—	92.5	252	514	133	647
16	Tula Oblast	25.7	2,361	1,622	—	95.2	220	454	103	557
17	Yaroslavl Oblast	36.4	3,427	1,339	—	95.2	356	679	71	750
18	City of Moscow	1.0	13,350	10,407	—	84.8	1,808	2,661	105	2,766

North-West Federal Okrug

19	Republic of Karelia	172.4	3,801	703	12.0	76.6	306	673	146	819
20	Republic of Komi	415.9	6,102	996	25.2	59.6	578	1,084	63	1,147
21	Arkhangelsk Oblast	410.7	3,499	1,263	–	94.2	243	609	218	826
22	Nenets AO	176.7	36,885	42	18.7	62.4	4,701	6,835	83	6,918
23	Vologda Oblast	145.7	5,481	1,245	–	96.6	597	945	52	997
24	Kaliningrad Oblast	15.1	2,986	945	–	82.4	299	640	196	835
25	Leningrad Oblast	85.3	4,483	1,653	–	89.6	440	781	71	852
26	Murmansk Oblast	144.9	5,702	873	–	85.2	491	997	271	1,268
27	Novgorod Oblast	55.3	3,183	674	–	93.9	282	540	139	679
28	Pskov Oblast	55.3	1,964	737	–	94.3	166	388	185	572
29	City of St. Petersburg	0.6	5,066	4,600	–	84.7	1,138	1,690	110	1,801
	South Federal Okrug									
30	Republic of Adygeya	7.6	1,306	445	24.2	64.5	68	196	291	487
31	Republic of Dagestan	50.3	1,274	2,622	29.4	4.7	35	92	301	392
32	Ingush Republic	4.3	535	482	77.3	1.2	12	55	452	507
33	Kabarda-Balkar Republic	12.5	1,432	897	67.0	25.1	103	199	271	469
34	Republic of Kalmykia	76.1	1,170	290	53.3	33.6	172	311	300	611
35	Karachai-Circassian Republic	14.1	1,429	435	49.8	33.6	62	182	364	546
36	Republic of North Ossetia	8.0	1,534	704	62.7	23.2	76	245	371	616
37	Republic of Chechnya	15.0	704	1,141	93.5	3.7	29	118	935	1,053
38	Krasnodar Krai	76.0	2,530	5,100	–	86.6	249	491	112	603
39	Stavropol Krai	66.5	1,885	2,718	–	81.6	192	350	149	499
40	Astrakhan Oblast	44.1	2,474	998	–	69.7	236	461	135	595
41	Volgograd Oblast	113.9	2,713	2,655	–	88.9	267	474	96	570
42	Rostov Oblast	100.8	2,132	4,334	–	89.3	189	387	135	523

(continued)

Russian Federation's Constituent States: Basic Facts (Continued)

Map location	Constituent states	Area (1,000 sq.km.)	GDP (US$/per capita, 2005)	Population, (1000, 2006)	Title ethnicity[a] (% of total population, 2002)	Russians (% of total population, 2002)	Own subnational budget revenues (US$ per capita, 2006)	Own and assigned subnational budget revenues (US$ per capita, 2006)	Transfers from federal budget per capita (US$, 2006)	Total subnational budget revenues per capita[b] (US$, 2006)
Privolgskiy Federal Okrug										
43	Republic of Bashkortostan	143.6	3,261	4,079	29.8	36.3	382	644	134	778
44	Republic of Mari El	23.2	1,667	717	42.9	47.5	146	330	224	554
45	Republic of Mordovia	26.2	1,865	866	31.9	60.8	198	408	222	630
46	Republic of Tatarstan	68.0	4,513	3,769	52.9	39.5	425	736	154	890
47	Republic of Udmurtia	42.1	3,162	1,553	29.3	60.1	252	541	79	620
48	Chuvash Republic	18.3	1,869	1,299	67.7	26.5	192	381	179	561
49	Kirov Oblast	120.8	1,927	1,461	–	90.8	171	392	171	563
50	Nizhny Novgorod Oblast	74.8	3,024	3,445	–	95.0	305	579	74	653
51	Orenburg Oblast	124.0	3,482	2,150	–	73.9	323	570	62	632
52	Penza Oblast	43.2	1,814	1,423	–	86.4	144	312	215	527
53	Perm Krai[b]	160.6	4,285	2,770	–	–	–	–	–	–
	Perm Oblast	127.7	–	2,637	–	85.2	448	770	45	815
	Komi-Perm AO	32.9	–	133	59.0	38.2	89	218	751	969
54	Samara Oblast	53.6	4,383	3,201	–	83.6	439	761	42	803
55	Saratov Oblast	100.2	2,253	2,626	–	85.9	174	352	124	476
56	Ulianovsk Oblast	37.3	2,146	1,351	–	72.6	184	363	211	574
Ural Federal Okrug										
57	Kurgan Oblast	71.0	1,774	992	–	91.5	133	300	214	515
58	Sverdlovsk Oblast	194.8	3,795	4,428	–	89.2	431	787	52	840

59	Tyumen Oblast	161.8	9,441	1,316	–	71.6	3,004	4,549	50	4,599
60	Khanty-Mansi AO	523.1	33,408	1,469	1.9	66.1	2,189	3,244	–114	3,130
61	Yamal-Nenets AO	750.3	29,183	523	5.2	58.8	2,939	4,648	45	4,693
62	Chelyabinsk Oblast	87.9	3,447	3,551	–	82.3	366	651	64	715
	Sibir Federal Okrug									
63	Republic of Altai	92.6	1,647	204	30.6	57.4	146	372	995	1,367
64	Republic of Buryatia	351.3	2,701	969	27.8	67.8	199	441	396	837
65	Republic of Tyva	170.5	1,303	308	77.0	20.1	58	219	711	930
66	Republic of Khakassia	61.9	2,689	541	12.0	80.3	246	510	115	625
67	Altai Krai	169.1	1,816	2,565	–	92.0	109	275	256	531
68	Krasnoyarsk Krai	2,339.7	5,283	2,925	–	–	755	1,153	167	1,320
	Krasnoyarsk Krai	710.0	5,285	2,868	–	88.9	–	–	–	–
	Tajmyr AO	862.1	4,830	39	21.5	58.6	–	–	–	–
	Evenk AO	767.6	5,943	18	21.5	61.9	–	–	–	–
69	Irkutsk Oblast	767.9	3,689	2,545	–	–	–	–	–	–
	Irkutsk Oblast	745.5	3,812	2,411	–	89.9	338	654	139	793
	Ust-Orda Buryat AO	22.4	1,488	134	39.6	54.4	56	201	617	818
70	Kemerovo Oblast	95.5	3,625	2,855	–	91.9	413	759	85	844
71	Novosibirsk Oblast	178.2	3,157	2,662	–	93.0	359	643	94	737
72	Omsk Oblast	139.7	3,815	2,047	–	83.5	294	565	207	772
73	Tomsk Oblast	316.9	5,316	1,037	–	90.8	467	835	113	948
74	Zabajkalsk Krai	431.5	2,194	1,136	–	–	–	–	–	–
	Chita Oblast	412.5	2,235	1,062	–	89.8	176	464	333	797
	Aginsk-Buryat AO	19.0	1,614	74	62.5	35.1	8,126	8,334	591	8,925
	Far-East Federal Okrug									
75	Republic of Sakha (Yakutia)	3,103.2	6,773	951	45.5	41.2	867	1,488	750	2,237
76	Primorski Krai	165.9	3,248	2,036	–	89.9	228	551	236	787

(continued)

Russian Federation's Constituent States: Basic Facts (*Continued*)

Map location	Constituent states	Area (1,000 sq.km.)	GDP (US$/per capita, 2005)	Population, (1000, 2006)	Title ethnicity[a] (% of total population, 2002)	Russians (% of total population, 2002)	Own subnational budget revenues (US$ per capita, 2006)	Own and assigned subnational budget revenues (US$ per capita, 2006)	Transfers from federal budget per capita (US$, 2006)	Total subnational budget revenues per capita[b] (US$, 2006)
77	Khabarovsk Krai	788.6	3,968	1,420	–	89.8	398	848	193	1,041
75	Amur Oblast	363.7	3,023	887	–	92.0	241	573	317	890
79	Kamchatka Krai	472.3	4,340	352	–	–	–	–	–	–
	Kamchatka Oblast	170.8	4,086	328	–	80.9	240	933	898	1,831
	Koryak AO	301.5	7,906	24	26.7	50.6	528	1,611	7,668	9,280
80	Magadan Oblast	461.4	5,221	175	–	80.2	420	1,285	949	2,234
81	Sakhalin Oblast	87.1	7,998	532	–	84.3	584	1,399	333	1,733
82	Jewish Autonomous Oblast	36.0	2,690	189	1.2	89.9	206	463	470	934
83	Chukotka AO	737.7	8,774	51	23.5	51.9	1,173	2,704	4,438	7,142

Source: Authors' calculations based on Federal State Statistics Service, 2004, 2007b; Ministry of Finance 12-month consolidated budget execution reports on January 1, 2007.

a. Title ethnicity is the indigenous ethnicity of an ethnic autonomy.

b. Because of the transitional period, statistical data are presented separately for most of the merging regions (Perm Krai, Krasnoyarsk Krai, Irkutsk Oblast, Zabajkalsk Krai, and Kamchatka Krai). Budget revenues for Krasnoyarsk Krai include data on Tajmyr and Evenk Autonomous Okrug (AO).

Appendix B

Map of the Russian Federation

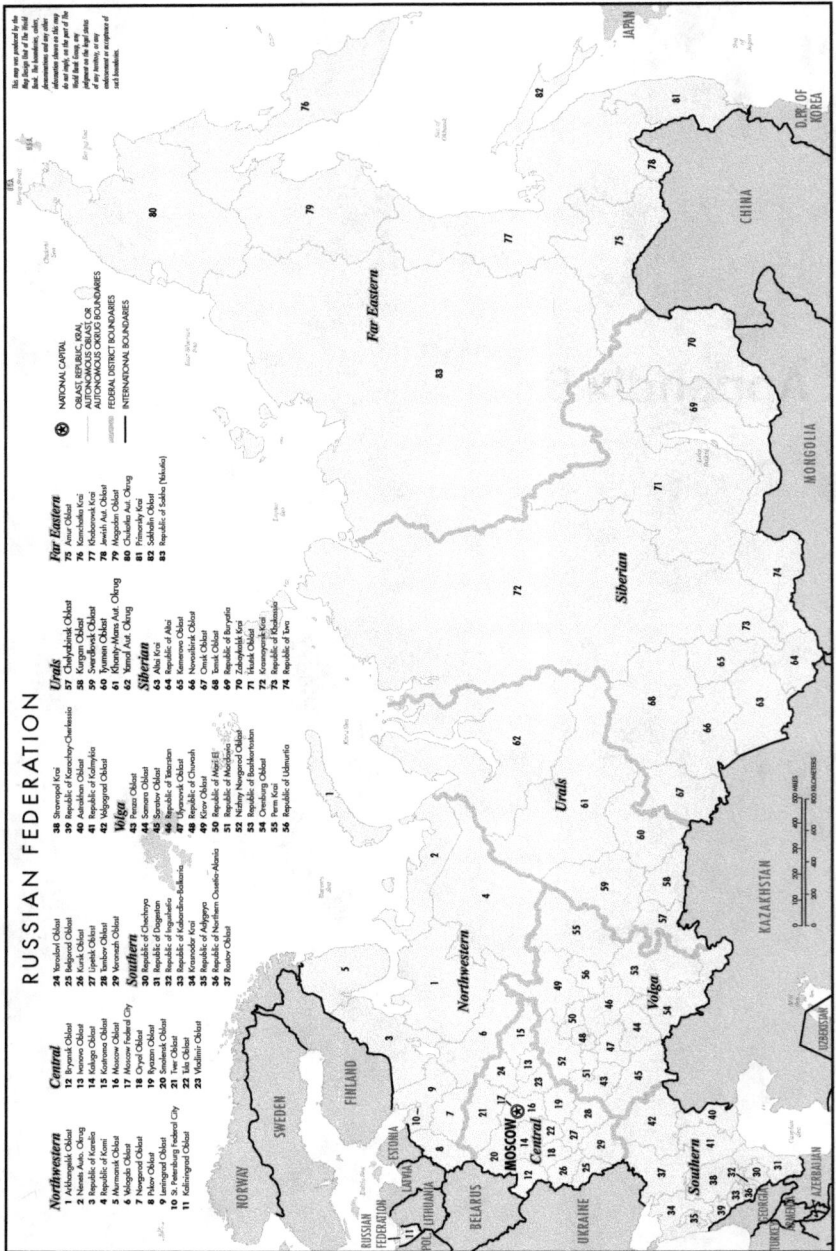

RUSSIAN FEDERATION

Legend

⊕ NATIONAL CAPITAL
OBLAST, REPUBLIC, KRAI, AUTONOMOUS OBLAST, OR AUTONOMOUS OKRUG BOUNDARIES
FEDERAL DISTRICT BOUNDARIES
INTERNATIONAL BOUNDARIES

Northwestern
1 Arkhangelsk Oblast
2 Nenets Auto. Okrug
3 Republic of Karelia
4 Republic of Komi
5 Murmansk Oblast
6 Vologda Oblast
7 Novgorod Oblast
8 Pskov Oblast
9 Leningrad Oblast
10 St. Petersburg Federal City
11 Kaliningrad Oblast

Central
12 Bryansk Oblast
13 Ivanovo Oblast
14 Kaluga Oblast
15 Kostroma Oblast
16 Moscow Oblast
17 Moscow Federal City
18 Oryol Oblast
19 Ryazan Oblast
20 Smolensk Oblast
21 Tver Oblast
22 Tula Oblast
23 Vladimir Oblast
24 Yaroslavl Oblast
25 Belgorod Oblast
26 Kursk Oblast
27 Lipetsk Oblast
28 Tambov Oblast
29 Voronezh Oblast

Southern
30 Republic of Chechnya
31 Republic of Dagestan
32 Republic of Ingushetia
33 Republic of Kabardino-Balkaria
34 Krasnodar Krai
35 Republic of Adygeya
36 Republic of Northern Ossetia-Alania
37 Rostov Oblast
38 Stavropol Krai
39 Republic of Karachay-Cherkessia
40 Astrakhan Oblast
41 Republic of Kalmykia
42 Volgograd Oblast

Volga
43 Penza Oblast
44 Samara Oblast
45 Saratov Oblast
46 Republic of Tatarstan
47 Ulyanovsk Oblast
48 Republic of Chuvash
49 Kirov Oblast
50 Republic of Mari El
51 Republic of Mordovia
52 Nizhny Novgorod Oblast
53 Republic of Bashkortostan
54 Orenburg Oblast
55 Perm Krai
56 Republic of Udmurtia

Urals
57 Chelyabinsk Oblast
58 Kurgan Oblast
59 Sverdlovsk Oblast
60 Tyumen Oblast
61 Khanty-Mansi Aut. Okrug
62 Yamal Aut. Okrug

Siberian
63 Altai Krai
64 Republic of Altai
65 Kemerovo Oblast
66 Novosibirsk Oblast
67 Omsk Oblast
68 Tomsk Oblast
69 Republic of Buryatia
70 Zabaykalski Krai
71 Irkutsk Oblast
72 Krasnoyarsk Krai
73 Republic of Khakassia
74 Republic of Tuva

Far Eastern
75 Amur Oblast
76 Kamchatka Krai
77 Khabarovsk Krai
78 Jewish Aut. Oblast
79 Magadan Oblast
80 Chukotka Aut. Okrug
81 Primorsky Krai
82 Sakhalin Oblast
83 Republic of Sakha (Yakutia)

Map labels: NORWAY, SWEDEN, FINLAND, ESTONIA, LATVIA, LITHUANIA, POLAND, BELARUS, UKRAINE, RUSSIAN FEDERATION, GEORGIA, AZERBAIJAN, KAZAKHSTAN, UZBEKISTAN, MONGOLIA, CHINA, D.P.R. OF KOREA, JAPAN, MOSCOW

District labels: Northwestern, Central, Southern, Volga, Urals, Siberian, Far Eastern

References

Ahmad, Ehtisham, Raju Singh, and Mario Fortune. 2004. "Toward More Effective Redistribution: Reform Options for Intergovernmental Transfers in China." IMF Working Paper 04/98, International Monetary Fund, Washington, DC.

Alam, Asad, Stepan Titov, and John Petersen. 2004. "Russian Federation." In *Subnational Capital Markets in Developing Countries: From Theory to Practice*, ed. Mila Freire and John Peterson with Marcela Huertas and Miguel Valadez, 571–91. New York: Oxford University Press.

Alexeev, Michael, and Galina Kurlyandskaya. 2003. "Fiscal Federalism and Incentives in a Russian Region." *Journal of Comparative Economics* 31 (1): 20–33.

Bahl, Roy. 1999. "Implementation Rules for Fiscal Decentralization." Working Paper 99-01, Andrew Young School of Policy Studies, Georgia State University, Atlanta.

Bahl, Roy, and Johannes F. Linn. 1992. *Urban Public Finance in Developing Countries*. Washington, DC: Oxford University Press.

Bahl, Roy, and Christine I. Wallich. 1995. "Intergovernmental Fiscal Relations in the Russian Federation." In *Decentralization of the Socialist State: Intergovernmental Finance in Transition Economies*, ed. Richard M. Bird, Robert D. Ebel, and Christine I. Wallich. Washington, DC: World Bank.

Bardhan, Pranab, and Dilip Mookherjee. 1998. "Expenditure Decentralization and the Delivery of Public Services in Developing Countries." Working Paper 90, Institute for Economic Development, Boston University, Boston, MA.

Bardhan, Pranab, and Dilip Mookherjee. 2006. *Decentralization and Local Governance in Developing Countries: A Comparative Perspective.* Cambridge, MA: MIT Press.

Bardhan, Pranab. 2002. "Decentralization of Governance and Development." *Journal of Economic Perspectives* 16 (4):185–205.

Bird, Richard M. 2000. "Rethinking Subnational Taxes: A New Look at Tax Assignment." *Tax Notes International* 20 (19): 2069–96.

Bird, Richard M., and Robert Ebel, eds. 2007. *Fiscal Fragmentation in Decentralized Countries: Subsidiarity, Solidarity, and Asymmetry.* Cheltenham, U.K., and Northhampton, MA: Edward Elgar.

Bird, Richard M., Robert D. Ebel, and Christine I. Wallich, eds. 1995. *Decentralization of the Socialist State: Intergovernmental Finance in Transition Economies.* Washington, DC: World Bank.

Bird, Richard M., and Andrey V. Tarasov. 2002. "Closing the Gap: Fiscal Imbalances and Intergovernmental Transfers in Developed Federations." Working Paper 02-02, Andrew Young School of Policy Studies, Georgia State University, Atlanta.

Bird, Richard M., and François Vaillancourt, eds. 2006. *Perspectives on Fiscal Federalism.* Washington, DC: World Bank.

Blanchard, Oliver, and Andrei Shleifer. 2000. "Federalism with or without Political Centralization: China versus Russia." NBER Working Paper 7616, National Bureau of Economic Research, Cambridge, MA.

Boadway, Robin, Sandra Roberts, and Anwar Shah. 1994. "The Reform of Fiscal Systems in Developing and Emerging Market Economies: A Federalism Perspective." Policy Research Working Paper 1259, World Bank, Washington, DC.

Break, George F. 1967. *Intergovernmental Fiscal Relations in the United States.* Washington, DC: Brookings Institution.

Brennan, Geoffrey, and James Buchanan. 1980. *The Power to Tax: Analytical Foundations of a Fiscal Constitution.* Cambridge, U.K.: Cambridge University Press.

Burki, Shahid Javed, Guillermo Perry, and William R. Dillinger. 1999. *Beyond the Center: Decentralizing the State.* Washington, DC: World Bank.

Che, Jiahua, and Yingyi Qian. 1998. "Insecure Property Rights and Government Ownership of Firms." *Quarterly Journal of Economics* 113 (2): 467–96.

De Figueiredo, Rui J. P., and Barry R. Weingast. 2001. "Constructing Self-Enforcing Federalism in the Early United States and Modern Russia." Haas School of Business and Department of Political Science, University of California at Berkeley, Berkeley, CA. http://politicalscience.stanford.edu/faculty/documents/weingast-constructing%20self-enforcing%20federalism. pdf.

de Tocqueville, Alexis. 1904. *Democracy in America*. New York: D. Appleton.

Dillinger, William, and Steven B. Webb. 1999. "Fiscal Management in Federal Democracies: Argentina and Brazil." Policy Research Working Paper 2121, World Bank, Washington, DC.

Dolinskaya, Irina. 2001. *Transition and Regional Inequality in Russia: Reorganization or Procrastination?* Washington, DC: International Monetary Fund Institute.

Ebel, Robert, and Serdar Yilmaz. 2002. "On the Measurement and Impact of Fiscal Decentralization." Policy Research Working Paper 2809, World Bank, Washington, DC.

Federal State Statistics Service. 2004. *All-Russia Population Census*. Moscow: Federal State Statistics Service. http://www.perepis2002.ru.

———. 2005. *Development of Local Self-Government in the Russian Federation*. Moscow: Federal State Statistics Service.

———. 2007. *Regions of Russia*. Moscow: Federal State Statistics Service.

Fiszbein, Ariel. 1997. "The Emergence of Local Capacity: Lessons from Colombia." *World Development* 25 (7): 1029–43.

Freinkman, Lev, and Alexander Plekhanov. 2009. "Fiscal Decentralization in Rentier Regions: Evidence from Russia." *World Development* 37 (2): 503–12.

Frye, Timothy, and Andrei Shleifer. 1997. "The Invisible Hand and the Grabbing Hand." *American Economic Review* 87 (2): 354–58.

Gaidar, Yegor. 1996. *Russian Economy in 1995: Tendencies and Perspectives* [in Russian]. Moscow: Institute for the Economy in Transition.

García, Beatriz Carrillo. 2008. "China's Fiscal Decentralization: Consequences for the Promotion of Local Development." *México y la Cuenca del Pacífico* 11 (31): 13–34.

Harber, Stephan, Douglass North, and Barry Weingast. 2003. "If Economists Are So Smart, Why Is Africa So Poor?" *Wall Street Journal*, July 30, A12.

IMF (International Monetary Fund). 2001. *Government Finance Statistics Manual*. Washington, DC: IMF.

Information Science for Democracy Foundation. 2005. "Diagnostics of Corruption in Russia: 2001–2005." Information Science for Democracy Foundation, Moscow. http://www.indem.ru.

Jarocińska, Elena. 2008. "Are Intergovernmental Grants Tactical? The Evidence from Russia." CASE Network Studies and Analyses 361, Center for Social and Economic Research, Warsaw.

Kelly, Lidia. 2009. "Russia Warns of Budget Cuts," *Wall Street Journal*, May 26.

Khaleghian, Peyvand. 2003. "Decentralization and Public Services: The Case of Immunization." Policy Research Working Paper 2989, World Bank, Washington, DC.

Kurlyandskaya, Galina. 2001. "Budgetary Pluralism of Russian Authorities." Local Government and Public Service Reform Discussion Paper 17, Local Government Initiative of the Open Society Institute, Budapest.

Kurlyandskaya, Galina, and Alexander Deryugin. 2007. "Fiscal Federalism in the Russian Federation." In *The Practice of Fiscal Federalism: Comparative Perspectives*, ed. Anwar Shah, 235–61. Montreal and Kingston, ON: McGill-Queen's University Press.

Kurlyandskaya, Galina, and Natalia Golovanova. 2006. "Decentralization in the Russian Federation." *Economic Change and Restructuring* 39 (3): 213–33.

Kurlyandskaya, Galina, Yelena Nikolayenko, and Natalia Golovanova. 2001. "Local Governments in the Russian Federation." In *Developing New Rules in the Old Environment: Local Governments in Eastern Europe, Caucasus, and Central Asia*, ed. Victor Popa and Igor Munteanu, 161–264. Budapest: Local Government Initiative of the Open Society Institute.

Lavrov, Alexei. 1998. *Intergovernmental Fiscal Relations in Russia: An Agenda for Reforms*. Moscow: Presidential Administration.

Le Houerou, Philippe. 1994. "Decentralization and Fiscal Disparities among Regions in the Russian Federation." Internal Discussion Paper 138, World Bank, Washington, DC.

Litvack, Jennie I. 1994. "Regional Demand and Fiscal Federalism." In *Russia and the Challenge of Fiscal Federalism*, ed. Christine Wallich, 218–40. Washington, DC: World Bank.

Martinez-Vazquez, Jorge. 2002. "Asymmetric Federalism in Russia: Cure or Poison?" Working Paper 03-04, Andrew Young School of Policy Studies, Georgia State University, Atlanta.

———. 2007. "Revenue Assignment in the Practice of Fiscal Decentralization." Working Paper 07-09, Andrew Young School of Policy Studies, Georgia State University, Atlanta.

Martinez-Vazquez, Jorge, and Jameson Boex. 2001. *Russia's Transition to a New Federalism*. Washington, DC: World Bank.

Martinez-Vazquez, Jorge, and Robert M. McNab. 2003. "Fiscal Decentralization and Economic Growth." *World Development* 31 (9): 1597–616.

Martinez-Vazquez, Jorge, Andrey Timofeev, and Jameson Boex. 2006. *Reforming Regional-Local Finance in Russia*. Washington, DC: World Bank.

McKinnon, Ronald. 1997. "Market-Preserving Fiscal Federalism in the American Monetary Union." In *Macroeconomic Dimensions of Public Finance: Essays in Honour of Vito Tanzi*, ed. Mario I. Blejer and Teresa Ter-Minassian, 73–93. London and New York: Routledge.

McLure, Charles E. 1994a. "The Sharing of Taxes on Natural Resources and the Future of the Russian Federation." In *Russia and the Challenge of Fiscal Federalism*, ed. Christine Wallich, 181–217. Washington, DC: World Bank.

―――. 1994b. "The Tax Assignment Problem: Ends, Means, and Constraints." *Australian Tax Forum* 11 (2): 153–83.

―――. 1995. "Comment on 'Fiscal Federalism and Decentralization: A Review of Some Efficiency and Macroeconomic Aspects.'" In *Annual World Bank Conference on Development Economics 1995*, ed. Michael Bruno and Boris Pleskovic, 317–22. Washington, DC: World Bank.

―――. 1998. "The Tax Assignment Problem: Conceptual and Administrative Considerations in Achieving Subnational Fiscal Autonomy." Paper prepared for the Intergovernmental Fiscal Relations and Local Financial Management Course, organized by the World Bank Institute, the Fiscal Affairs Division of the Organisation for Economic Co-operation and Development, and Georgia State University, Vienna, March 16–27.

Musgrave, Richard A. 1959. *The Theory of Public Finance: A Study in Public Economy*. New York: McGraw-Hill.

―――. 1983. "Who Should Tax, Where, and What?" In *Tax Assignment in Federal Countries*, ed. Charles E. McLure, 97–122. Canberra: Center for Research on Federal Financial Relations.

Nee, Victor, and Sijin Su. 1996. "Institutions, Social Ties, and Credible Commitment: Local Corporatism in China." In *Reforming Asian Economies: The Growth of Market Institutions*, ed. John McMillan and Barry J. Naughton, 111–34. Ann Arbor: University of Michigan Press.

North, Douglass. 1990. *Institutions, Institutional Change, and Economic Performance*. Cambridge, U.K.: Cambridge University Press.

North, Douglass, and Barry Weingast. 1989. "Constitutions and Commitment: The Evolution of Institutions Governing Public Choice in Seventeenth-Century England." *Journal of Economic History* 49 (4): 803–32.

Oates, Wallace E. 1972. *Fiscal Federalism*. New York: Harcourt Brace Jovanovich.

OECD (Organisation for Economic Co-operation and Development). 1999. "Taxing Powers of State and Local Government." Tax Policy Study 01, OECD, Paris.

Polishchuk, Leonid. 2000. "Legal Initiatives in Russian Regions: Determinants and Effects." Center for Institutional Reform and the Informal Sector, University of Maryland, College Park, MD.

Popov, Vladimir. 2004. "Fiscal Federalism in Russia: Rules versus Electoral Politics." *Comparative Economic Studies* 44 (4): 515–41.

Powell, Bill. 2008. "Just How Scary Is Russia?," *Fortune*, September 15.

Prud'homme, Remy. 1995. "The Dangers of Decentralization." *World Bank Research Observer* 10 (2): 201–20.

Rao, Govinda M., and Raja J. Chelliah. 1991. *Survey of Research on Fiscal Federalism*. New Delhi: National Institute of Public Finance and Policy.

Rao, Govinda M., and Nirvikar Singh. 2005. *Political Economy of Federalism in India*. New Delhi: Oxford University Press.

Rossi, Marco. 1998. "Decentralization: Initial Experience and Expectations of the SDC." Swiss Agency for Development and Cooperation, Bern.

Shah, Anwar. 1994. *The Reform of Intergovernmental Fiscal Relations in Developing and Emerging Market Economies*. Washington, DC: World Bank.

———. 1998. "Balance, Accountability, and Responsiveness: Lessons about Decentralization." Policy Research Working Paper 2021, World Bank, Washington, DC.

———. 2004. "Fiscal Decentralization in Developing and Transition Economies: Progress, Problems, and the Promise." Policy Research Working Paper 3282, World Bank, Washington, DC.

Shah, Anwar, Theresa M. Thompson, and Heng-Fu Zou. 2004. "The Impact of Decentralization on Service Delivery, Corruption, Fiscal Management, and Growth in Developing and Emerging Market Economies: A Synthesis of Empirical Evidence." CESifo DICE Report 1/2004, *Journal for Institutional Comparisons* 2 (1): 10–14.

Shleifer, Andrei, and Daniel Treisman. 2000. *Without a Map: Political Tactics and Economic Reform in Russia*. Cambridge, MA: Massachusetts Institute of Technology.

Stepan, Alfred C. 1999. "Federalism and Democracy: Beyond the U.S. Model." *Journal of Democracy* 10 (4): 19–34.

Strumpf, Koleman S. 1999. "Does Government Decentralization Increase Policy Innovation?" Department of Economics Working Paper, University of North Carolina, Chapel Hill, NC.

Tanzi, Vito. 1995. "Fiscal Federalism and Decentralization: A Review of Some Efficiency and Macroeconomic Aspects." In *Annual World Bank Conference on Development Economics 1995*, ed. Michael Bruno and Boris Pleskovic, 295–316. Washington, DC: World Bank.

Ter-Minassian, Teresa, ed. 1997. *Fiscal Federalism in Theory and Practice*. Washington, DC: International Monetary Fund.

Thiessen, Ulrich. 2005. "Fiscal Federalism: Normative Criteria for Evaluations, Developments in Selected OECD Countries, and Empirical Evidence for Russia." Discussion Paper 518, German Institute of Economic Research, Berlin.

Tiebout, Charles. 1956. "A Pure Theory of Local Public Expenditures." *Journal of Public Economy* 64 (5): 416–24.

Treisman, Daniel. 1996. "The Politics of Intergovernmental Transfers in Post-Soviet Russia." *British Journal of Political Science* 26 (3): 299–335.

Treisman, Daniel. 2007. *The Architecture of Government: Rethinking Political Decentralization*. Cambridge, U.K.: Cambridge University Press.

Wallich, Christine I., ed. 1994. *Russia and the Challenge of Fiscal Federalism*. Washington, DC: World Bank.

Weingast, Barry. 1995. "The Economic Role of Political Institutions: Market Preserving Federalism and Economic Development." *Journal of Law, Economics, and Organization* 11 (1): 1–18.

Wong, Christine C. P., and Richard M. Bird. 2005. "China's Fiscal System: A Work in Progress." Working Paper 05-20, Andrew Young School of Policy Studies, Georgia State University, Atlanta.

World Bank. 1996. *Fiscal Management in Russia*. Washington, DC: World Bank.

———. 2000. *World Development Report 1999/2000: Entering the 21st Century*. New York: Oxford University Press.

———. 2001. "Decentralization and Governance: Does Decentralization Improve Public Service Delivery?" PREM Notes 55, World Bank, Washington, DC.

Yakovlev, Evgeny, and Ekaterina Zhuravskaya. 2006. "State Capture: From Yeltsin to Putin." Working Paper 94, Center for Economic and Financial Research at New Economic School, Moscow. http://www.cefir.ru.

Yusuf, Shahid. 2009. *Development Economics through the Decades: A Critical Look at 30 Years of the World Development Report*. Washington, DC: World Bank.

Zhuravskaya, Ekaterina V. 2000. "Incentives to Provide Local Public Goods: Fiscal Federalism, Russian Style." *Journal of Public Economics* 76 (3): 337–68.

Zhu, Jieming. 2004. "Local Developmental State and Order in China's Urban Development during Transition." *International Journal of Urban and Regional Research* 28 (2): 424–47.

Index

Boxes, figures, notes, and tables are indicated by b, f, n, and t, respectively.

fiscal decentralization/political
recentralization (1999–2001),
28–29t, 37–39
fiscal recentralization (2005–08), 29t,
46–47, 47–48t
formalization of rules (1994–1998),
28t, 34–37
local and regional governments,
relationship between
1990–2005, 85–90
2006-present, 90–94, 92–94f, 92t
main stages of, 28–29t
spontaneous decentralization (1991–93),
28t, 30–34, 30f
horizontal fiscal [im]balance, 12–13, 14t,
61–62
housing and utilities expenditures, 51,
56t, 58t
Hungary, 34n8

I

IGFR. *See* intergovernmental reform in
Russian Federation
IMF (International Monetary Fund), 3n2
in-kind benefits, 37–38
in-kind payment of taxes, 27
India, 33n6, 102, 107n5
Indonesia, 107n5
industry, uneven distribution of, 2, 21
Information Science for Democracy
Foundation, 106
inframarginal funding, 61
Ingush Republic, 21n3, 22, 111t
institutions, intergovernmental,
design of. *See* design,
intergovernmental
intergovernmental reform in Russian
Federation, ix–x
authoritarianism and
centralization/decentralization,
links between, 26
basic facts and statistics about
constituent states, 110–14t
centralization. *See* centralization
decentralization. *See* decentralization
design of, 49–98. *See also* design,
intergovernmental
federal structure, 17–24, 18f, 19b
federalism in Russia, current
and future state of, 99–108.
See also federalism in Russia

fiscal decentralization, 1–15. *See also*
fiscal decentralization
history of, 25–48. *See also* history of
intergovernmental relations in
Russian Federation
map of regional governments, 115–16f
mergers of subjects, 22–24, 23t, 53
Putin administration, 8b, 38, 97, 100
size and diversity of Russia, 1–2, 15,
20–22, 78
subnational governments. *See* local
governments; subjects of the
federation
International Monetary Fund (IMF), 3n2
intraregional fiscal decentralization, 13n11
Irkutsk Oblast, 23t, 113t, 115–16t

J

Jarocińska, Elena, 35, 36n10

K

Kaliningrad Oblast, 84t, 111t, 115–16t
Kalmykia, 67, 73, 81b, 111t, 115–16t
Kalmyks, 22
Kamchatka Oblast and Kamchatka Krai,
22, 23t, 114t, 115–16t
Karachai-Circassian Republic, 23, 111t,
115–16t
Karelia, 32, 111t, 115–16t
Khabarovsk Krai, 86b, 114t, 115–16t
Khaleghian, Peyvand, 3n2, 5
Khanty-Mansi Autonomous
Okrug, 21, 23–24, 85, 104,
113t, 115–16t
Komi-Permyatsky Autonomous
Okrug, 22, 23t, 84n16,
112t, 115–16t
Korea, Republic of, 8b
Koryak Autonomous Okrug, 22, 23t, 76b,
83t, 84n16, 114t, 115–16t
Kozak, Dimitry, and Kozak's reforms,
39n12
krais, 20, 53, 63. *See also* subjects of the
federation
Krasnodar Krai, 22, 111t, 115–16t
Krasnoyarsk Krai, 22, 23t, 76b, 82, 83t, 90,
95, 103, 113t, 115–16t
Krasnoyarski Raion, 92
Kuril Islands, 84t
Kurlyandskaya, Galina, xiv, 39, 40, 67, 89,
99n, 106